# WITH GLOWING HEARTS

*How Ordinary Women
Worked Together to
Change the World
(And Did)*

Winner of the Best of the Fest Award,
2016 Saskatoon Fringe Festival

Selected for the 2018 Words by Women Week,
Urban Stages, New York

## PRAISE FOR
## *WITH GLOWING HEARTS*

"A stirring underdog story."

– CAM FULLER, *StarPhoenix*

"The biggest winner was *With Glowing Hearts*…a triumph for Jennifer Wynne Webber."

– NED POWERS, *Saskatoon Express*

"Beautifully researched, Jennifer has written a poignant and timely play about four working class women in a mining town who decide to take action. Fighting to build unions and fighting towards a common good are alien concepts in the early 21st century, but *With Glowing Hearts* reminds us that we stand on the shoulders of ordinary women who worked to build a better, fairer world for us."

– COLLEEN MURPHY, playwright & two-time recipient of the Governor General's Literary Award for Drama

"Your heart will glow with pride in our history and fill with hope for our future. A 'must see' for everyone – whether you are a social activist or not. Go celebrate this true story and leave inspired and challenged. I laughed and cried. I got angry. I gained courage. I was challenged by the lives lived. I saw the connections between yesterday and today. I am more hopeful than ever that together we can make our lives, our communities, our country and our world a better place for all."

– BARB BYERS, Member of the Order of Canada & former Secretary-Treasurer of the Canadian Labour Congress

"This play is just what you'll need to lift your hearts and your spirits! What an inspiring story about how a small group of brave women organized to bring change for all workers! Such an important part of the history of workers' safety and workers' rights."

– LORI JOHB, President of the Saskatchewan Federation of Labour

"If your emotions aren't stirred by Webber's *With Glowing Hearts* I'd bet you've a heart of stone. With a spirited mix of hardship, humour, role playing, and song, four feisty female characters take on the Big Bosses of the Kirkland Lake gold mining community. Red-baiting, government surveillance, and company-funded violence only spurs them on, with past and present merging as the women relive an historic 1941 strike and the subsequent events. Their actions will birth the Canadian wing of the International Mine Mill & Smelter Workers' Union Ladies Auxiliary dedicated to social change and justice for workers and their families. *With Glowing Hearts* throws theatrical light on a little known Canadian story and its unsung heroes. *With Glowing Hearts* – a dramatic delight on multiple levels, entertaining, engaging and enlightening."

– SHARON POLLOCK, playwright & two-time recipient of the Governor General's Literary Award for Drama

"A spare, sensitively written and beautifully paced script. Jennifer Wynne Webber knows what specific personal details to include and precisely when a moment of humour is needed and she gives each of the characters a strong individual voice."

– IAN C. NELSON, director, dramaturge, playwright

"Superb… so moving some in the audience were weeping, and yet it's a beautifully uplifting story… I don't like this star system, but if we must have it, this play definitely deserves five stars."

– RUTH MILLAR, author, librarian, historian

Also by
Jennifer Wynne Webber

BOOKS
*Defying Gravity* (2000, novel)
*Beside Myself* (2001, play)


ONLINE PUBLICATIONS
*Criatura* (2007, short story)
*White Lies* (2014, play)

# WITH GLOWING HEARTS

*How Ordinary Women
Worked Together to
Change the World
(And Did)*

*To Katelyn,
With all best wishes,
Jennifer*

Jennifer Wynne Webber

*Great to meet you!*

*With Glowing Hearts:*
*How Ordinary Women Worked Together to Change the World (And Did)*
first published 2019 by Scirocco Drama
An imprint of J. Gordon Shillingford Publishing Inc.
© 2019 Jennifer Wynne Webber

Scirocco Drama Editor: Glenda MacFarlane

Cover design by Doowah Design

Cover photo and page 23: *"Two-mile demonstration of support by wives and children of striking Kirkland Lake miners,"* City of Greater Sudbury Heritage Images, Solski Collection, ID# MK2344

Author photo by Jonathan Forrest.

Production photos from video by:
J. W. Webber (TheatreOne production); S.E. Grummett (Obiz production)

Epigraph from *THEOPHILUS NORTH* by Thornton Wilder Copyright © 1973 by The Wilder Family LLC. Reprinted by arrangement with The Wilder Family, LLC and The Barbara Hogenson Agency, Inc. All rights reserved.
*To read more about Thornton Wilder, go to* www.ThorntonWilder.com

"Union Maid" lyrics by Woody Guthrie, 1940. This song entered the public domain in Canada in 2018. For performances outside Canada, a performance licence would likely be required. For more information see: Woody Guthrie Publications & TRO-Ludlow Music, Inc(BMI) at www.woodyguthrie.org

Printed and bound in Canada on 100% post-consumer recycled paper.

We acknowledge the financial support of the Manitoba Arts Council and The Canada Council for the Arts for our publishing program.

For production inquiries please visit: www.jenniferwebber.com

*Library and Archives Canada Cataloguing in Publication*

Title: With glowing hearts : how ordinary women worked together to change the world (and did) /
Jennifer Wynne Webber.
Names: Webber, Jennifer Wynne, author.
Description: A play.
Identifiers: Canadiana 2019006112X | ISBN 9781927922491 (softcover)
Classification: LCC PS8595.E26 W58 2019 | DDC C812/.6—dc23

J. Gordon Shillingford Publishing
P.O. Box 86, RPO Corydon Avenue, Winnipeg, MB Canada R3M 3S3

*To Jonathan,*

*for the glow in my heart,*

*for everything.*

*(Photo: Jonathan Forrest)*

# Jennifer Wynne Webber

Jennifer was born in Ottawa and now lives on Vancouver Island. She has also lived and worked in Montreal, Saskatoon, Calgary, and Edmonton.

Jennifer earned an Honours degree in History from the University of Saskatchewan before embarking on a varied and serendipitous career path. To date, this has included working as an oral historian, speechwriter, television journalist, professional actor, communications advisor, dramaturge, writing instructor, and video producer. She also devoted several years to taking full-time care of her mother, a time she cherishes as one of the most meaningful of her life.

Through it all, Jennifer has continued to write in multiple genres, earning an M.F.A. in Creative Writing from the University of British Columbia along the way.

Jennifer is the author of two other books: *Defying Gravity*, a novel which was nominated for three Saskatchewan Book Awards including Book of the Year; and *Beside Myself*, a play critically praised as "compelling," "impassioned and intelligent." Two of her plays have been presented as staged readings in New York at the Off-Broadway, Obie Award–winning theatre Urban Stages: *With Glowing Hearts* and *White Lies* (under its former title *Whistling at the Northern Lights*). In 2007, the latter play was also chosen as one of Canada's top five new plays for Germany's *Neue Theaterstücke aus Kanada*, a playwriting competition juried in Berlin. *White Lies* was later published in the online literary journal *Ryga: A Journal of Provocations*.

Jennifer is married to artist Jonathan Forrest to whom she is grateful for their very happy life together and for their shared determination to keep walking the artistic path, eyes open to the delights all around them, every step of the way.

# Acknowledgments

Many hands touch a play as it is helped along its way. Here is my best effort to acknowledge those helping hands.

This new, full-length play grew from a shorter one-act play commissioned in early 2015 by University of Saskatchewan (U of S) professor Dr. Elizabeth Quinlan, a woman of warmth, wit, good cheer, and true collegial spirit who has remained a key supporter of the whole unfolding project ever since. Thank you, Liz, for everything and, above all, for your friendship.

I am also grateful to the talented cast and whole intrepid team in Saskatoon who signed on to mount that original production of the one-act play in 2016, as well as to the U of S Departments of Sociology and of Drama, to assistant project manager Susan Robertson, and to Marion Hooge, Beverley Kobelsky, Gail Lasiuk, Carla Orosz, Doug Thorpe, and Andrea Quinlan for all their efforts and expertise.

Funding for the original play's research and development was provided by the Social Sciences and Humanities Research Council (SSHRC). This SSHRC support included funding for a key five-day developmental workshop in Saskatoon in April 2016.

Two readings in Nanaimo were also helpful to the play's development. The very first draft of the play received a half-day workshop in Nanaimo in January 2016. Thank you to TheatreOne for giving us the space and to actors Michelle Lieffertz, Nicolle Nattrass, Erin Ormond, and Sharon Wahl. Nanaimo's Western Edge Theatre also presented a staged reading of the one-act version in November 2016. Thank you to Frank Moher, Brian March, director Clarice McCord and actors Sheridan Collyer-Vallens, Jocelyn Dickson, Barbara Metcalfe, and Susan Warner.

My gratitude also goes to the remarkable team assembled for the extensive workshop and staged reading at Lunchbox Theatre's *2017 Stage One Festival of New Work* – a terrific experience all round – and to the Stage One Reading Committee for choosing the play in the first place: Mark Bellamy, Samantha MacDonald, Karen Johnson-Diamond, Valmai Goggin, and Trevor Rueger.

Just prior to rehearsals for the TheatreOne production, Working Class Theatre in Victoria, BC held an informal public reading of the all-new, full-length version of the play as part of its Jazz Page reading series in March 2018. For that, I thank Tristan Bacon, David Elendune, and actors Kaitlin Blackwood, Natasha Guerra, Joanna James, and Rae Paxton.

Heartfelt thanks to David Mann, Artistic Director of Nanaimo's TheatreOne, who in 2017 encouraged me to write the full-length version of the play and then promptly "set the stage" for a premiere production. Thank you for assembling such a glowing-hearted cast and crew. My thanks as well to TheatreOne's hard-working board; Eliza Gardiner; Nadine Wiepning; Serena Hartel for her work as design assistant; and Charlie Angus, NDP Member of Parliament for Timmins-James Bay, for allowing the theatre to play his song and video, "*Having to Say Goodbye*" (recorded by the *Grievous Angels*), prior to the show each night.

Special thanks to Frances Hill, Artistic Director of Urban Stages in New York, for once again showing enthusiastic support for my work and for mounting a staged reading of the play in late April 2018, which was invaluable for making further script refinements – and a rollicking good time. Three cheers to the stellar cast and the entire Urban Stages team.

I am very grateful to the late Mike Solski, and to his daughter Sandra Spratt, for collecting and safeguarding so many of the remarkable photographs and other historical records that helped to inspire this play. I also thank the very helpful staff of the Ontario Archives, the Laurentian University Archives, UBC Rare Books and Special Collections, and the Greater Sudbury Public Library.

For their assistance in locating additional photographs and other materials, I also thank David Crouch of Kirkland Lake, Kelly Gallagher from Kirkland Lake's Museum of Northern

History, and, especially, Kate Lasiuk, who made two trips to the Ontario Archives on a last ditch – and very productive – hunt for some missing photographs that I am delighted to include in this book. Thanks too to the Ukrainian Canadian Research and Documentation Centre, especially Andre Sochaniwsky and Bozhena Gembatiuk Fedyna, for helping me to learn more about the little known contribution of Ukrainian Canadians who served during World War II, which in turn helped me create the "backstory" for Poppy's brother.

I also thank Dr. Katharine Rollwagen of Vancouver Island University for her valuable advice on the final section of this book. My thanks as well to Dr. Mercedes Steedman, to Bob Miner (son of miner and union activist Bob Miner), and to the intrepid librarians at the Timmins Public Library, Kitchener Public Library, Cochrane Public Library, and Kirkland Lake's Teck Centennial Library for their assistance in helping me track down other key images and pieces of information for the historical section at the back of this book.

My gratitude also goes to all the glowing-hearted friends and family members who attended the play's performances and readings (sometimes travelling great distances to do so) and who offered me so much love, support, and encouragement, especially stalwart friends Kate Day and Lynn Guina who, on top of everything else, gave me food, drink, and beds to sleep on. Heartfelt hugs and raised glasses to you all.

My heart overflows when it comes to my remarkable, loving, and supportive sisters, Jill Webber Hrabinsky and Joan Webber. They, along with Jill's husband Robert Hrabinsky and their daughter (my beautiful niece) Sarah Hrabinsky, and Joan's husband Jason Proctor, each made special sacrifices to support my work on this play. My deepest thanks and love to every single one of you.

For all his thoughtfulness, love, and faith in me, I thank my husband, Jonathan Forrest. Walking this path with you is the joy of my life.

Finally, I wish to thank my extraordinary mother, Mona Marie (Haslett) Webber, the smart, resilient, optimistic, and ever-inspiring woman who, as a hard-working single mother, raised me and my sisters to see the beauty, hope, and possibility in everything around us. I so wish you might have lived to see this play on stage but I still feel you with me, still see you clapping your hands together when I read out the early drafts to you, still hear you saying – about those valiant women of Kirkland Lake – "They were amazing!" Yes, Mom, they were. But so were you and I could never have written this play without you.

With love and thanks,
Jennifer

# Production History

The full-length version of *WITH GLOWING HEARTS: How Ordinary Women Worked Together to Change the World (And Did)* premiered on April 11, 2018 at Nanaimo's TheatreOne on Vancouver Island.

DOROTHY MACFARLANE ..... Michelle Lieffertz

KAY CARSON ........................... Tamara McCarthy

POPPY CHYTUK ........................... Amber Landry

CÉCILE GAUTHIER ........................ Linda Pollard

David Mann – Director

Robin Boxwell – Production Manager & Sound Designer

Margaret Handford – Set, Costumes,
Props & Projections Designer

Robinson Wilson – Lighting Designer

David Baughan – Stage Manager

Jessica Schacht – Assistant Director

Gabrielle Marcon – Technical Assistant

The original one-act version of *WITH GLOWING HEARTS: How Ordinary Women Worked Together to Change the World (And Did)* previewed on June 13, 2016 at the Saskatchewan Federation of Labour's Prairie School for Union Women in Waskesiu, Saskatchewan and premiered on July 28, 2016 at the Saskatoon Fringe Festival where it was named Best of the Fest.

Produced by Elizabeth Quinlan (Obiz Productions) in collaboration with the University of Saskatchewan's Departments of Sociology and of Drama and funded by the Social Sciences & Humanities Research Council (SSHRC).

DOROTHY MACFARLANE ............... Erin Carson

KAY CARSON ........................... Caitlin Zacharias

POPPY CHYTUK ............................Rachelle Block

CÉCILE GAUTHIER ...........................Nadia Mori

Elizabeth Quinlan – Project Manager

Julia Jamison – Director

Jillian Borrowman – Stage Manager & Assistant Director

Jared Beattie & Logan Martin-Arcand – Set Design

Miranda Hughes – Costume Design

S.E. Grummett – Sound Design

The one-act version of *WITH GLOWING HEARTS: How Ordinary Women Worked Together to Change the World (And Did)* also received a four-day workshop at Lunchbox Theatre as part of the Stage One Festival of New Canadian Work. This culminated in a public reading on June 23, 2017 in Calgary, Alberta.

DOROTHY MACFARLANE ........ Kristen Padayas

KAY CARSON ................................. Cheryl Hutton

POPPY CHYTUK ................................. Amy Burks

CÉCILE GAUTHIER ...................... Valerie Planche

Valmai Goggin – Director / Dramaturge

Mark Bellamy – Lunchbox Artistic Producer & Festival Coordinator

Ailsa Birnie – Festival Assistant

*WITH GLOWING HEARTS: How Ordinary Women Worked Together to Change the World (And Did)* was chosen in 2018 for the Off-Broadway Words by Women Week at Urban Stages in New York. Urban Stages presented a staged reading of the full-length version of the play on April 26, 2018.

DOROTHY MACFARLANE ..... Valerie Terranova

KAY CARSON ........................... Stephanie Cozart

POPPY CHYTUK .......................... Lauren Schaffel

CÉCILE GAUTHIER .................... Stephanie Stone

Frances Hill – Artistic Director

Kim T. Sharp – Director

Antoinette Mullins – Development & Literary Director

Dorothy typing union propaganda. Seated: Dorothy (Erin Carson),
Standing, L–R: Kay (Caitlin Zacharias); Poppy (Rachelle Block); Cécile
(Nadia Mori). Saskatoon Fringe Festival, 2016.
*Photo from video by S.E. Grummett.*

The women play their miner husbands – and take liberties. L–R: Cécile
(Nadia Mori); Poppy (Rachelle Block); Kay (Caitlin Zacharias); Dorothy
(Erin Carson). Saskatoon Fringe Festival, 2016.
*Photo from video by S.E. Grummett.*

Sharing a laugh after singing Woody Guthrie's "Union Maid." L–R:
Cécile (Linda Pollard); Kay (Tamara McCarthy); Dorothy (Michelle
Lieffertz); Poppy (Amber Landry). TheatreOne production, 2018.
*Photo from video by J.W. Webber.*

On the march with the women of Kirkland Lake. L–R: Kay (Tamara
McCarthy); Dorothy (Michelle Lieffertz); Poppy (Amber Landry); Cécile
(Linda Pollard). TheatreOne production, 2018.
*Photo from video by J.W. Webber.*

Waiting for word at the mine-head. L–R: Poppy (Amber Landry); Cécile (Linda Pollard); Dorothy (Michelle Lieffertz); Kay (Tamara McCarthy). TheatreOne production, 2018.
*Photo from video by J.W. Webber.*

Seeing donations roll in from across the country. L–R: Dorothy (Michelle Lieffertz); Kay (Tamara McCarthy); Poppy (Amber Landry); Cécile (Linda Pollard). TheatreOne production, 2018.
*Photo from video by J.W. Webber.*

Poppy gets arrested, again. L–R: Dorothy (Michelle Lieffertz); Poppy (Amber Landry). TheatreOne production, 2018.
*Photo from video by J.W. Webber.*

Passing the torch. L–R: Cécile (Linda Pollard); Poppy (Amber Landry); Dorothy (Michelle Lieffertz); Kay (Tamara McCarthy). TheatreOne production, 2018.
*Photo from video by J.W. Webber.*

# Playwright's Notes

*Kirkland Lake Women's March*

From the moment I saw the photograph of the long line of women marching through the snow, they captured my heart – those determined women of Kirkland Lake.

They were walking at least two or three abreast in a line that stretched back two miles or so, maybe further. The line dissolved from view in a far-off blur of grey and white, where the snow and sky met amid the town's buildings away in the distance behind them.

These women were walking out of a time and place I couldn't quite see. Their faces were hard to read as well – some were stoic, seemingly expressionless, some may have been smiling but they might just as well have been grimacing against the cold. It was just too hard to see. Their faces were too small, the photograph itself too grainy.

But the strength of their intention was clear. These women were on the move.

In the photograph, they don't appear to be moving quickly. One at the front has her hands in her pockets while another carries a handbag and another, further back, holds the hand of a small child who is also trudging along, parka hood up, bundled against the cold. But their movement looks steady, resolute. These women are simply taking one step after another.

It felt like they had no intention of stopping – like they wanted to march right out of that frozen image and on into the present. I wanted to help them do it. And what a journey and privilege it has been to do so.

For that I am grateful to Dr. Elizabeth (Liz) Quinlan who brought her research on the Ladies Auxiliary union movement to my attention nearly four years ago and asked me to find a play inside it.

This play is based on that rich material – interview transcripts, decades of Ladies Auxiliary newsletters, academic articles, books, and compelling archival photographs such as the one of the Kirkland Lake women's march that caught my eye and my heart from the moment I saw it. All of this only made me hungry to know more and so I, in turn, began a hunt of my own for more historical treasures, particularly about the town and people of Kirkland Lake since they had so captured my imagination. But, as Liz also notes in her Foreword, the lack of historical documentation on the women I wanted to write about did not make that easy.

Another challenge was that what a playwright may need to create characters and scenes can require additional types of research. I had to get into the skin of these women and plant myself firmly into their world. To do so, I needed to find out such things as what, exactly, might go wrong with a wood-burning stove, just how you made a "mock" apple pie, what road it was the women marched and just why the locals called it the "Mile of Gold." I also had to understand how specific wartime events might have affected the women, such as how and where a young Ukrainian Canadian man (the fictional brother to Poppy) might have died in the war. All this required many a trip down many an additional research rabbit hole and, sometimes, casting my mind back to my own grandmothers and the stories passed down of the severe hardships they faced raising families with few resources during the late 1930s and early 1940s. And so this play also draws on all of that, as well.

But this is indeed a play, not a documentary. I have altered and compressed some events and melded various real people together with my own imaginings to create new, fictional characters. And what those characters do – and *why* they do what they do – is filtered and informed by my imagination and experience. And all this is then further rendered and shaped into a theatrical creation with its own demands for structure, logic, symmetry, and more.

Is this ultimately what the women of Kirkland Lake from 1941 would say and do if we could gather them together with us in the here and now? I don't know. But this script shows you what they did and what they said in my mind's eye when I invited them out of the old photograph. And now their march continues.

Scripts summon up new interpretations and discoveries every time people gather to play with them. And, when they do, individuals in every new audience watch and listen from different vantage points in time, space, and mind – and that affects what they see and what they hear. It's not a runaway train – there is a script to keep it on track, after all – but when it jumps aboard for that journey from page to stage, a play gains new meaning and momentum.

It's in that spirit that I hand over this story, these characters, to see what they may now become, in your minds, on your stages – with one final thought to share before you enter their world.

Many, possibly most, of the real women who gave their time and energy to union ladies auxiliary groups across the continent never had any idea what they accomplished. Maybe that's because grand gestures like the Kirkland Lake women's march were few and far between. Most of their work was modest and cumulative. They did what they could for as long as they could, even when they saw no sign of progress, never mind success, and even when they thought they'd lost utterly. Some went to their graves before labour laws changed in this country. Some saw conditions improve and laws change, but never realized how much their own seemingly small actions contributed to that change. Because of that, this play is also my heartfelt gift to the "Kirkland Lake gals of 1941" and all who followed in their footsteps – all those women who just kept putting one foot in front of the other. See what you did? You changed the world.

Jennifer Wynne Webber

# Foreword

During the winter of 1941–42, the temperatures in northern Ontario were bitingly cold, but the miners were on fire. Thirty-eight hundred miners struck against eight gold mines in Kirkland Lake for a full twelve weeks to press the mine owners to recognize and bargain with their union. The war years were a period of politicization amongst the working class. For workers in many industries, including the gold miners in northern Ontario, the hardships they faced during the Great Depression were fresh in their memories and cemented their determination to fight for better working and living conditions. The strike in Kirkland Lake was one of many strikes during the war and union membership doubled in Canada.

At the time of the gold miners' strike, there was no legislative requirement of companies to recognize unions, as had already been achieved in the United States in 1935. But the industrial unions forming in the United States were also gaining a foothold in Canada and, as a result, the Canadian workers were ignited by the potential the new structure of these unions offered them. They faced formidable foes in the capitalist class, including the mine owners in northern Ontario who were determined to prevent the industrial unions from making inroads into the mining communities. The owners defied the recommendations of the government conciliation board to bargain with the union and were prepared to starve the miners rather than have a successful union-organizing drive on their watch. Conflict in the relations between miners and their employers was never far from the surface in the mining camps throughout Canada, but the arrogance, malice, and inhumanity exhibited by the gold mine owners during the late 1930s and early 1940s generated a degree of defiance amongst even those miners who didn't ordinarily question the legitimacy of the owners' control. The treatment the miners received from the owners led many to militancy, although few were members of the Communist Party and even fewer cared that several of the union leaders were party members. Their militancy was shored up by a long-standing solidarity they enacted every day in the course of their exceptionally dangerous work. The idiom 'you watch my back and I'll watch yours' was not just a philosophical abstraction; it had the utmost practical importance for workers who entered the endlessly dark subterranean passageways to excavate precious metal from the guts of the earth where sudden cave-ins spelled crushing burials.

The police, Ontario Premier Hepburn's "Hussars," arrived in Kirkland Lake one week after the strike began and marched down the town's main street every morning. The federal government adopted a "no-interference" position that indirectly supported the owners; Prime Minister Mackenzie King refused to even meet with the union representatives. The mine owners lobbied for public support by filling the print media with anti-union propaganda. Conveniently, the *Globe and Mail* was owned by one of the mine-owners. The nation watched with bated breath as the struggle unfolded. Workers and capitalists alike recognized that a victory by this brazen mining union could spell subsequent victories achieved by other unions in other industries. A breakthrough achieved for the miners in Kirkland Lake would inspire other segments of the working class for whom collective bargaining had previously appeared equally hopeless.

The strike was lost, but it did, a year and half later, break the historic refusal of the government and the capitalist class to grant concessions to labouring people and their unions. Legislation similar to the U.S.'s Wagner Act was passed in 1944, introducing a new legalistic order governing labour relations in Canada. Much has been written about the Kirkland Lake strike because of its historical significance. It gave way to the government-enforced, employer recognition of unions that forms Canada's present-day codified system of industrial relations. Perhaps more importantly, the strike bolstered the self-confidence and organizing skills among the miners and, in doing so, played a decisive role in the development of industrial unionism in Canada. The overwhelming majority of the strikers were not rehired after the strike was called off, even though that violated the anti-discrimination clauses of the Criminal Code. So, these unemployed miners dispersed to other parts of the country where they could get work, primarily in the industrial centres such as Hamilton, Sudbury, and Sarnia. This distributed a large number of class-conscious workers, now with well-honed organizing skills and proficient in strike tactics, throughout the industries in Canada. Applying their newly developed expertise to large groups of unorganized workers, as they did, accelerated the growth of the industrial unions – precisely what the mine owners, and other Canadian capitalists, desperately wanted to avoid.

When I first learned about the strike, I immediately recognized its importance, having grown up in a union household and well aware of the challenges Canadian workers faced over the decades to secure better wages and safer working conditions. But, as a feminist, I had to wonder what was the role of women in the strike. The image of a wife standing behind her striking husband was a prominent theme in the labour movement in the 1940s. As a union newspaper described, "a good union gal worked to support her family, used makeup moderately, kept her stocking seams straight, and went out on the picket line with her man because having girls come on the line…puts more pep in the gas" (*CIO News*, Feb 20, 1939). Did the gold miners' wives in Kirkland Lake conform to this description? To be a hard rock miner was, and to some degree still is, to be a virile, masculine man, rugged as the ore he extracts, and much is known about the dangerous conditions miners faced in the course of their work. But, I wondered, what did it feel like for their wives to shoot dice with death each day their husbands went to work? An injury or, even worse, a fatality was economically devastating to the entire family, since in those one-industry mining towns, there were few jobs for women. How did the women distract themselves, hour by hour, as their husbands blasted, mucked, loaded, drilled in dirty, dank tunnels at the behest of employers who considered the price of life to be trivial? The strike, like many strikes, opened the eyes of workers to their place in the economic order and the nature of their relationship with the capitalist class. But, was there a similar awakening of the strikers' wives? Did they challenge the gender norms of the times? How did their involvement in the strike affect their subsequent activities?

It wasn't easy to investigate the story of the women of the Kirkland Lake strike. Most of the archival documents of the times track the activities, adversities, and accomplishments of men. The war offered significant opportunities to women to join the labour market as waged workers. But, because most women laboured in the home and the community without being compensated by a wage, their relationship to the formal institutions of the working class was seldom considered important enough to document. With so few archival materials, students of women's historical involvement in the labour movement are left to fill in the gaps between what is known about women's own distinctive culture and life experience and the existing descriptive labour histories of the time. Over a period of eight years, with support from the Social Sciences and Humanities Research Council, I scoured the available archival documents together with my research assistant and union sister, Gail Lasiuk, and my daughter Andrea Quinlan, who is a scholar in her own right. We owe a large debt of gratitude to the archivists at University of British Columbia Special Collections, Archives of Ontario, Laurentian University, and Library and Archives Canada. Piece by piece, we uncovered some of the little-known story of these women. What we came away with was far too enthralling to be left as an academic article that would most likely simply collect dust. I felt compelled to share my findings more widely. I chose to use drama as the medium because it has so many of the elements inherent in human communication – symbols, emotion, and performance. Jennifer Wynne Webber, the playwright, has done a superb job of dramatizing this honourable history of the "Kirkland Lake gals." She seamlessly integrates the historical material into the stories of four female characters, reflecting the ethnic, religious, and political diversity of the Kirkland Lake population, in a beautifully paced script stippled with precisely timed humorous moments and the evocative power of direct address, classic tableaux, and inventive yet simple dramatic punctuation. During the summer of 2016, the one-act version of the play toured Saskatchewan and received the Best of the Fest Award when it was performed at the Saskatoon Fringe Festival. Since, its full-length rendition has delighted audiences in Nanaimo, B.C. and a staged reading was performed in New York.

I am indebted to the Social Sciences and Humanities Research Council and the University of Saskatchewan for their funding of the development and production of the original one-act version of the play, which has since grown into the full-length play published here.

Elizabeth Quinlan
Department of Sociology
University of Saskatchewan
January, 2019

# Characters in Order of Appearance

### DOROTHY MACFARLANE
Early to mid 30s. Married to miner Jim MacFarlane.
Recently moved from Timmins. Somewhat of an
outsider, perhaps simply by nature, perhaps by
background. Also, the daughter of a miner.

### KAY CARSON
Mid to late 30s, possibly older. Married to miner
husband Bob Carson. Convent-educated Catholic.
Irish family background, although not necessarily
recent enough to have an accent.

### POPPY CHYTUK
The youngest of the bunch, possibly just 18.
Ukrainian Canadian, originally from Saskatchewan.
Newlywed, to Danny Chytuk, a Ukrainian
Canadian miner and former young hero of the
Estevan Coal Miners' Strike.

### CÉCILE GAUTHIER
Early 50s, which makes her both the eldest of
the women and a child of the previous century.
Mother of nine surviving children. (Her eldest son
is 31, her youngest daughter is not quite 10.)
Originally from Quebec (likely Val d'Or, but perhaps
from as far away as the Lac St. Jean region). Married
to Alphonse Gauthier, a miner promoted
to cage tender, for at least 32 years.

The women also play their own husbands and other characters
as noted in the script. When they do, they take liberties.

# Time and Place

Kirkland Lake, Ontario in 1941–42, and the present.

The present is simply the present moment the characters are sharing with the audience. (They do not become elderly.)

When they're in the present, they are not only well removed in time and space from the events of 1941–42 and able to think about that time in retrospect, they are well aware of the audience before them, of the fact that they are in a play, and, of the fact that there is a wider world beyond that of the play.

Some scenes are firmly rooted in one time or the other, others move more fluidly between the past and the present, sometimes with asides to the audience in the present, even as the events around them are occurring in 1941–42.

## Set

As minimal as can be, with boxes or other pieces used to create or hint at any furniture or locations needed. A clothesline or two. Even that much referred to typewriter of Dorothy's may not be physically needed…and may perhaps be even better conjured through typing actions and sounds.

The sheets the women hang up on the clothesline(s) could serve as screens if projections of scene titles and/or archival photographs are used – but, if so, sheets of various sizes could catch partial, fragmented images – there's no need for the sheets to be too literally "screen" like. The sheets may also become other things as needed, such as the strike tents and, later in the play, possibly even the paper streaming from Dorothy's typewriter.

## Archival Images

While projections of archival photographs and other images are referred to throughout the play, it is entirely possible to stage the play without using projections. There are many images available for use, however, if desired.

## Music

While only one song is specifically called for within the action of the play (preferably Woody Guthrie's "Union Maid"), other songs could potentially be sung before or after the play, and possibly at the act-break if one is taken. If that is done, you might wish to consider: "Mining for Gold" (Traditional / James Gordon / Philip Thomas); "Having to Say Goodbye" (Charlie Angus); "Bread and Roses" (Mimi Fariña / James Oppenheim).

*(Please note, however, that if this is done, these additional songs should be kept outside the action of the play itself, occurring clearly before or after the play, and not as part of it.)*

## Note on the Story

While this play is inspired by true events and real people, characters, names, incidents, and events have been altered and fictionalized for dramatic purposes.

*"The past and the future are always present within us."*

—Thornton Wilder

# ACT ONE

## Scene 1: ORDINARY WOMEN

> *DOROTHY MACFARLANE scrolls a fresh piece of paper into her typewriter.*
>
> *As she looks at it, her old friends emerge from her mind's eye...and she may turn to watch them.*
>
> *They hang sheets on clotheslines – which may soon be used as screens for projections of archival photos and the text DOROTHY will type.*
>
> *DOROTHY speaks to the audience.*

DOROTHY: When I picture us all, back then, I can still hardly believe it. Who did we think we were? I mean, we weren't the kind of people who could change things. Bunch of miners' wives. About as ordinary as you can get. Mind you, we did have Kay, Kay Carson.

> *KAY CARSON, 36, hears her name. Now at her typewriter, DOROTHY types out KAY's name.*

She knew what needed doing. Without Kay, none of this would have happened – and I wouldn't be who I am.

KAY:  Oh, go on with ya. I never dreamed we'd upset the apple cart, either. I was a convent-raised girl at heart – was, is, and always will be. No, I was just someone who tried to accept things as they were. Like my husband liking his drink a little too much. Like not being able to have a baby. I'd learned to make do, get on with life. I was no firebrand. I was no – Poppy.

*POPPY CHYTUK ties a kerchief over her hair turban-style, then applies some lipstick.*

DOROTHY:  (*Typing the name.*) Poppy Chytuk. (*"Chytuk" is pronounced "CHIH-tuk."*) Her real name was Pavla – Ukrainian. Poppy was a nickname but we probably should have called her "Hellzapoppin" 'cause she was something.

POPPY:  Hell, all I wanted back then was lipstick that would stay on even after a good smooch. Mind you, it was a bit of a kick sending my hubby off to work, him never dreaming he had a big red clown face on him. "No, hon, no lipstick on ya' – you're good." (*Laughs.*) Naw, as far as I was concerned, I was the girl who had it all: when you moved to town, Dorothy, I'd been married six months to the cutest hubby in the world and already had a sneakin' suspicion company was comin.' That's all I was thinkin' about. (*She taps her belly.*)

*CÉCILE GAUTHIER finishes murmuring a rosary in French.*

CÉCILE:  *"...Sainte Marie, Mère de Dieu, priez pour nous pécheurs, maintenant, et à l'heure de notre mort. Amen."*

DOROTHY:   (*Typing the name.*) Cécile Gauthier. You'd think a person just couldn't be as sweet as Cécile was – that people like that were only in movies like *Song of Bernadette* – but you'd be wrong. You'd also be wrong to think "sweet" means "pushover." Cécile was as strong as they come.

CÉCILE:   *Non, non,* I had to pray and pray for strength. Me, I was a sinner. We are all such sinners. My good mother always said: when you start thinking that's not true, that maybe you're not so bad after all, that's when you're *really* in trouble! So I prayed all the time to *La Vierge,* our Mother in Heaven, to help me – keep helping me and my whole family, all my nine children *et mon époux* Alphonse – to stay true to the one true faith. Because who I was back then, who I am, is a faithful person – (*Catching herself.*) – and such a sinner.

   *POPPY blasts out a laugh.*

DOROTHY:   So that was us, a bunch of –

KAY:   Wait. You're forgetting somebody. You! (*Waving DOROTHY to type.*) Dorothy MacFarlane.

DOROTHY:   (*Typing her name.*) Well, I truly was the last person who'd want to look for trouble. After all the hard times we'd had, I was just so grateful Jim had found a job again. I needed him to hang on to it – and not just for us, either. My dad, back in Timmins, he had silicosis in his lungs and my sister was an invalid too, so we had to send whatever we could to help them out. We were in no position to stick our necks out. Though I will say, I'd have done just about anything to make a friend in town – I'll give you that. But, that was us. A bunch of perfectly ordinary women who were –

CÉCILE:        Sinners.

DOROTHY:       – the last people to go around stirring up
               trouble.

POPPY or ALL:  The Kirkland Lake gals of 1941!

DOROTHY:       Kirkland Lake, Ontario. A little gold mining
               town perched atop the solid rock of the
               Canadian Shield.

KAY:           Though how solid was it, really? With all those
               mine shafts carved through it.

POPPY:         Hundreds of them.

CÉCILE:        Like open lace cutwork – miles below our feet.

DOROTHY:       Up on the surface, we tried not to think about
               that.

               *They feel the ground shift beneath their feet as a
               deep rumble sounds.*

               Rock burst.

KAY:           They also called 'em bumps. Which doesn't
               sound so bad, does it?

POPPY:         That's the company for you. Downplaying it.

DOROTHY:       They happened all the time.

CÉCILE:        But they could be so dangerous.

POPPY:         It was like our men were going off to war every
               single day.

DOROTHY:       And, in a way, they were. Gold was vital to the
               war effort.

CÉCILE:        An essential industry.

KAY:           So our men were doing their bit, here on the
               home front.

POPPY:    And a deadly front it was. Each and every day, we never knew if they'd come back.

*Another low rumble as they feel another small tremor…*

DOROTHY:    Put solid rock under enough pressure –

KAY:    Think solid glass cube held tight in a vice. More than twenty-seven thousand pounds of pressure.

DOROTHY:    – and eventually it'll shatter.

KAY:    And we don't mean just a crack here and there or a little piece or two breaking off,

POPPY:    We mean shatter.

DOROTHY:    A whole slab or part of the rock ceiling.

KAY:    All coming down at once.

CÉCILE:    Crashing down, hard.

KAY:    Tons and tons of rock.

CÉCILE:    Before it would happen, the men would hear it snap, *hein?* Snap, snap, snap.

KAY:    That's the rock talking.

POPPY:    It's when you don't hear it talking, you get worried.

KAY:    That means the pressure's really building up.

CÉCILE:    And, when it talks again, that's it. Sounds like a pistol shot.

*A loud pistol-like sound. The women flinch.*

KAY:    Above ground, you'd feel a tremor. Like a little earthquake.

CÉCILE:         You'd feel it right in your bones.

DOROTHY:        And you'd stop. One question in your mind:

KAY:            Would there be a siren or not?

                *They wait, listening for a siren that does not
                sound.*

DOROTHY:        Then you'd go on with your day. Doing
                whatever you did.

                *Still speaking to the audience, we see them start
                to get back to their work: KAY, picking up her
                husband's clothes; DOROTHY typing, CÉCILE
                praying, POPPY attempting housework.*

KAY:            Picking up after the fella.

DOROTHY:        Typing letters home, to my dad and sister back
                in Timmins.

CÉCILE:         I'd be praying I was wrong, that it was just a
                heavy truck in the road.

POPPY:          I'd be trying to get my blasted housework done,
                dancing to the radio all the while.

DOROTHY:        That was us all over, wasn't it? Chipper enough
                on the surface –

CÉCILE:         Terrified down below.

                *The ground beneath them shifts again as another
                low rumble sounds…*

                *After again stopping to listen for a siren, they pick
                up their tasks again, pursuing them with extra
                fervour…*

                *They are now fully immersed in their old lives…
                in Kirkland Lake, 1941.*

> *DOROTHY pounds the typewriter keys; POPPY dances through her housework; CÉCILE prays harder than ever; KAY goes to pick something else off the floor – and stumbles on one of her husband's gigantic slippers.*

KAY:    Oh, for the love of – you'd think Bob was trying to kill me. Method of murder: booby trap. I've had it with these slippers – and everything else of his lying all over the blessed place!!

> *A siren blasts. The women stop cold. There is a moment as CÉCILE crosses herself and KAY hugs her husband's slippers to her chest. Then…*

POPPY:    Oh no, you don't. Oh, no, no, no, no you don't, you SON OF A BITCH!!!

> *At that POPPY and the other women break off at a run, KAY still clutching her husband's slippers.*

**Scene 2:**     CRUSHING TRUTHS

> *At the mine-head. (If projections are used, the women might emerge from an archival photo of a crowd at a mine-head.)*

> *CÉCILE, POPPY, and KAY rush to each other. DOROTHY stands somewhat apart from the rest.*

POPPY:     How bad is it? Do they know yet?

KAY:     They're still trying to tack their way through to the men. Mine manager's only saying –

POPPY:     Lemme guess: "Calm down, ladies. We've got it under control." Like hell.

CÉCILE:     Have a little faith.

POPPY:     In what? The company?

> *DOROTHY steps toward the other women.*

DOROTHY:     Any word on…

KAY:     No news. Haven't got through to them yet.

DOROTHY:     Over there. Looks like something's happening. Should someone go ask?

KAY:     No point going over. They just told us to stay put.

DOROTHY:     But –

POPPY:     Oh, they'll let us know what's happening "as soon as there's anything to know." Bloody hell.

DOROTHY:     But those are company men, right? All gathered, over there. *(Motioning.)* It really does look like there's something happening there now.

KAY:            It does.

DOROTHY:        So it'd be worth someone asking the mine manager again, then, wouldn't you think?

POPPY:          Oh, you'd think.

CÉCILE:         You're not from around here.

DOROTHY:        No. How did –

KAY:            It's just, they hate us to bother them at a time like this.

POPPY:          No. Wouldn't want them to be bothered by a bunch of annoying little women. Why would we have a right to know who's trapped down there? Whether they're alive or – we're only the BLOODY WIVES!!!!

CÉCILE:         *Calme-toi*, Poppy. The men in charge know best, I'm sure.

POPPY:          Oh Cécile, you can't believe that.

DOROTHY:        She's right, you know. We really should be able to –

POPPY:          See! I'm right. We should bloody force them to talk to us!

CÉCILE:         *Non, non, non*, Poppy. *Reste-ici.*

KAY:            *(To DOROTHY.)* You're not helping things.

POPPY:          Oh, yes she is! Cécile, let me go – I'm going to have a word with those BASTARDS!

                *CÉCILE holds POPPY back.*

CÉCILE:         Poppy goes over there, there'll be injuries for sure.

KAY:  Fine. I'm going, I'm going. For all the good it'll do. (*She starts off, then looks back.*) Well, aren't you coming? It's your bright idea, after all.

*KAY sets off at a clip. DOROTHY follows. They near a crowd of men.*

Now, there's the mine manager, over there. Talking to the hoistman. As soon as he's done, you get in there and talk to him.

DOROTHY:  Me? No, I can't. I can't talk to a man like that.

KAY:  No one can talk to a man like that.

DOROTHY:  No, I mean I really can't. I can't get the words out.

KAY:  You're getting them out fine.

DOROTHY:  No, in front of men. I can't speak up in front of men like that.

KAY:  Well, you'll have to. He won't want to talk to me. I'm Kay, by the way. Kay Carson.

DOROTHY:  Dorothy – MacFarlane.

KAY:  MacFarlane? You're husband's Jim?

DOROTHY:  That's right.

KAY:  Well, he's been working with my Bob this last while. You're from Timmins, aren't you? You two don't have kids, either, do you?

DOROTHY:  No, never blessed with – not so far.

KAY:  It can be hard around here, without kids. You'll have to come round for coffee.

| | |
|---|---|
| DOROTHY: | Why, I'd love to. I'll admit I've been lonesome. The only people we knew here were Betty and Wally Floody. They moved here from Timmins when we did – but they've left. Wally signed up and is overseas now, flying Spitfires. Betty's back at her parents. She's got to be just terrified, him flying around in fighter planes over there. |
| KAY: | You think that's any more dangerous than working in the mines these days? Honestly. There's been, what, three cave-ins just since you got here? Was it this bad in Timmins? |
| DOROTHY: | No better, I don't think. Two more men were killed there the very day we left. *(Looking over at the mine manager.)* Looks like they're almost done talking, doesn't it? |
| KAY: | Not quite, I don't think. |
| DOROTHY: | Wish that was our old manager back in Timmins. He was good to my dad. And his wife was the most lovely, lovely person. We were sure sorry when they left town. The new manager was an ornery son of a gun. |
| KAY: | Well, that's this fella all over. Brace yourself. |
| DOROTHY: | Why won't he want to talk to you? |
| KAY: | He already has, for one thing, and he told me we have to wait. For another, I think he suspects my Bob's one of the fellas starting to agitate. |
| DOROTHY: | Agitate? For a union? |
| KAY: | Well, not for a picnic, that's for sure. |

DOROTHY:     A picnic might do more good.

             *KAY gives her a look.*

             I just mean, aren't things tough enough
             already? All pushing for a union's going to do
             is lose men their jobs.

KAY:         That's what I thought – but Bob doesn't think
             it'll come to that. Besides, he says better their
             jobs than their lives. And at this point, I'm
             inclined to – hey, they're done talking. Get in
             there. Go on with you.

             *KAY steps back. DOROTHY musters the courage
             to talk to the mine manager.*

DOROTHY:     Excuse me. Sir?

             *KAY motions for DOROTHY to move closer.
             DOROTHY is invisible to the mine manager for
             some time.*

             Sorry to bother you, sir, at a time like this, but…
             my husband's one of the, um…I realize you'd
             inform us if…but could you just – oh sorry, am
             I in the way? Oh, of course. We'll wait.

             *She returns to KAY.*

             Sorry. You were right. There was no point me
             trying, that's for sure. Not with the way I clam
             up.

KAY:         No, you did as well as I could have. And it was
             worth the try. Reminds 'em we're still here.

             *DOROTHY and KAY rejoin the others.*

POPPY:       Don't tell me. The little ladies are supposed to
             sit tight and wait.

KAY:         That's about it.

*A shift as they address the audience in the present, even as they wait just as they did in 1941.*

DOROTHY:  *(To audience.)* So that's what we did. Waited.

*They wait.*

And waited.

*They shift positions and wait again.*

KAY:  And I mean we were prepared to wait, and all.

POPPY:  But there's waiting and then there's just being left dangling. Mine manager never did come back with any word.

DOROTHY:  We had to wait four more hours until the next shift came off, but then –

*A shift fully back into 1941.*

CÉCILE:  Alphonse! *(Waving.)* Alphonse! *Grâce à Dieu.* He's okay!

POPPY:  Thank God.

KAY:  Cécile's husband is a cage tender.

DOROTHY:  So he'll know –

KAY:  He'll know whatever there is to know.

*CÉCILE becomes ALPHONSE.*

CÉCILE
as ALPHONSE:  *Oui, encore de rock burst, hein?* This time, forty-four hunnerd feet down. Some of the guys were heading in when it happened. Couple got out by the man-way but the rest were blocked, *hein?* So we got guys trapped in there, nine of them. But we hear them tapping, *hein?* So we got some two-inch pipe shoved through to them. Got candles to them. But, some bad injuries, for sure.

*ALPHONSE pauses.*

KAY:              It's Bob, isn't it? He's –

CÉCILE
as ALPHONSE:  Aw Kay, yeah, he's trapped in dere but he's okay
              – at least so far. When it come crashing down,
              he's on the udder side with some guy name Jim,
              Jim Mac – MacDonald, Mac-*quelque chose?*

DOROTHY:       MacFarlane.

CÉCILE
as ALPHONSE:  *Oui,* dat's right! Dat's…ah okay, I'm sorry dere,
              *madame. Mon Dieu.* But him and Bob, dey're
              not so bad as de udder ones, *non.* Not like…ah,
              *hostie.* Poppy.

POPPY:         No. Oh, no bloody way, nooo –

CÉCILE
as ALPHONSE:  Dan's alive, okay. Still alive, Poppy. But him
              and two other guys near the back face, dey're
              pinned unner rock there, pretty bad. They don't
              know if…

              *KAY grabs POPPY.*

KAY:           He's alive. That's all that matters. That's all we
              think about right now.

DOROTHY:       How close are they to getting them out?

CÉCILE
as ALPHONSE:  Rescue team is down there, hard at it. Trouble
              is…

POPPY:         What?

CÉCILE
as ALPHONSE: The smoke is getting through, *hein?* The rest of the mine's still going full tilt, of course, so the men there, the trapped men, they sent a message to tell the company to shut 'er down – stop the smoke from choking them in there.

DOROTHY: So they have, then? Stopped?

KAY: Of course they have. Haven't they?

*ALPHONSE looks at them.*

POPPY: You got to be kidding! This is…it's…

CÉCILE
as ALPHONSE: Hey, hey, hey, *restez-calme, là. La compagnie,* no, she's not gonna to stop for dat, no way. But mine rescue team, *là?* Doze guys'll get 'em out. You'll see.

*ALPHONSE removes his helmet and becomes CÉCILE again. CÉCILE reaches for POPPY to comfort her.*

CÉCILE: You'll see. There, there. Oh, Poppy. Come sit. *Viens avec moi.*

*POPPY and CÉCILE sit down.*

KAY: They'll be okay.

DOROTHY: They've got to be.

KAY: They're alive – and they got word out.

DOROTHY: They did, but –

KAY: I mean, that's something. Everything.

DOROTHY: You're right. I'm sure you're right.

KAY:          And when Bob is up and at 'em again, I'm going to bowl him right over. I'm going to support him all the way. 'Cause he's right. It is time for a union.

DOROTHY:      Well, I...

KAY:          And he'll get no more arguments from me on the subject, just you see. It's too long we've let the company have all the power when it's our men down there putting their lives on the line every single day. There's a man killed in the mines every week in this province so...no. No, no, no, no, no. *(Increasingly wound up.)* It's time to say no to all that and it's time to work together. Stick together. Let the company know they have to start making conditions safer and paying fair wages or the workers that keep the mine going just won't do it anymore. They won't.

DOROTHY:      Are you all right?

KAY:          Of course, I am, I...and once we're through this, the company'll have to pay attention. Because we're strong. All we have to do is stay strong and not let anything shake us, shake our resolve – oh no...

              *KAY starts looking around her.*

DOROTHY:      What's the matter?

KAY:          I've dropped one.

DOROTHY:      One?

KAY:          I just had it. One of his slippers. I was holding them when... Oh no, oh how silly. I don't even know why I was still holding them. Or why I... but where could...oh no...

DOROTHY:      It's all right – there it is! See? *(Picking it up.)* Kay, it's right here. It's okay.

*As DOROTHY hands it to her, KAY breaks down.*

KAY:              It's so silly. It's just a slipper. It's...

DOROTHY:          It's his.

                  *KAY nods and surprises DOROTHY by hugging
                  her hard.*

                  *They shift back into the present...*

                  *CÉCILE and POPPY rejoin KAY and DOROTHY.*

KAY:              You know, I'd forgotten how silly I got.

POPPY:            You think that's silly? Should have seen me at
                  the hospital. Oh wait – ya did!

CÉCILE:           *(Crossing herself.)* Two of the men died down
                  there.

DOROTHY:          That day was just...that whole night...

KAY:              My Bob wore those slippers again, though. I got
                  him back.

DOROTHY:          You did. I got Jim back too. Barely a scratch on
                  him. Nine lives, I swear. That man.

POPPY:            Danny made it out too, but I'd never seen him
                  like that. He was so...broken. I didn't know
                  what I was going to do.

CÉCILE:           We were so worried about you.

DOROTHY:          That's what sparked it all.

KAY:              It was. But if it weren't for you, Dorothy, it sure
                  never would have caught fire. Literally.

                  *They share a smile as DOROTHY picks up a basket
                  of biscuits for the next scene, moving into 1941
                  once again.*

## Scene 3: LIGHTING THE FIRE

> *KAY's house. She's blowing into a wood-burning kitchen stove that just won't light. A knock at the door.*

KAY:            Oh for Heaven's sakes. Come on you, blankety-blank stove! Light!

> *She tries to use her apron to fan the would-be flames.*

DOROTHY:     *(Offstage.)* Hello?

KAY:            Come on in, whoever you are!! I can't get the door!

> *DOROTHY enters carrying the basket.*

DOROTHY:     Oh dear. Need a hand? *(She coughs at the smoke.)* I brought some biscuits.

KAY:            Oh, you're a godsend! Bob has some men coming over this morning from the union and here I didn't have a thing to feed them. Thanks to this blasted stove.

DOROTHY:     There's already a union here?

KAY:            Mine, Mill and Smelter Workers Union. Local 240. *("240" is pronounced "two-forty.")* There's only been a few of them kicking around with it but Bob wants to make a real push with it now. Oh! *(Coughs again at the smoke.)* Honestly, I don't know what the devil is up with this. Went out again right after I made the coffee. The vents are all skewgee or something. *(Skewgee is pronounced "skew-jee.")*

DOROTHY:     Ours is like that. I could try to…

KAY:    Please. Have at it!

*KAY takes the biscuits and has a look at them while DOROTHY tries her hand at lighting the stove.*

Bob usually finds a way to jimmy it, but of course he's still recovering. We can't afford to get it fixed properly. And this smoke is all he needs.

*She tries to wave away the smoke.*

DOROTHY:    How's he doing?

KAY:    Back in bed at the moment – which is good. He's limping something fierce, though he swears nothing's broken. Not that he'll let me call a doctor. Doesn't want those bills on top of it all.

DOROTHY:    That's my Jim all over.

KAY:    He's okay, though?

DOROTHY:    Seems to be. I just wish a doctor could have a listen to his lungs. When he takes a deep breath, it sounds like bagpipes in the distance –

KAY:    That droning –

DOROTHY:    Exactly – and that was before being trapped in all that smoke.

KAY:    That McIntyre Powder the companies make 'em inhale now – have you noticed it helping Jim yet?

DOROTHY:    Not really. Seems so strange, too. Breathing in aluminum dust to protect against the other dust.

KAY:    Well, it's supposed to coat the lungs, so maybe it'll take time for there to be an effect.

DOROTHY:    Maybe. Yeah, maybe it'll do something over time.

            *DOROTHY finishes with the stove.*

KAY:        Hey! You got it going! Thank you!

            *KAY goes to pour a couple of coffees.*

DOROTHY:    Oh, you're welcome. Glad I could help. Say, any more news on Poppy's husband?

KAY:        He's still in hospital. He's going to make it, but they don't know if he'll lose the arm. Poppy was in bad shape when I left – she's still there waiting, God help her. Cécile's with her now. On top of it all, she's expecting. Just found out.

            *A beat.*

DOROTHY:    If he can't work again, would there be any compensation?

KAY:        If he loses the arm. If he's not found at fault for anything. You know how it goes. Anyway, I've been thinking…

DOROTHY:    When I say that my husband gets nervous.

            *They share a chuckle.*

KAY:        Thing is, it's wrong Poppy could be left with nothing. I hate to say it but, the way things are, she could be better off if he did lose the arm. Then at least she'd get something. But if he pulls through as a cripple and can't work? There she'll be, with a babe-in-arms and a bunch of whopping hospital bills. What's she going to do then? There's no jobs here for women.

DOROTHY:    Does she have any family who can help?

KAY: Not a one. She's from all the way out in Saskatchewan so she never did have anyone here, but they're all gone anyway. Her mom died, having Poppy. Her dad died in Thirty-Seven, after they lost the farm. Then, last year, she loses her only brother. His ship makes it through the evacuation of Dunkirk only to sink later that same month. *HMCS Fraser.* Cécile says Poppy adored him.

DOROTHY: Dear Lord.

KAY: So, it's down to us. We've got to step up and help her.

DOROTHY: A gal like Poppy – would she even accept charity?

KAY: Would a hungry mother-to-be refuse a hot meal set in front of her? A few baby clothes from her sisters? Because that's what we are, you know, her sisters. We're her family now.

DOROTHY: Well, Poppy's a dear. Everybody will want to pitch in to help her.

KAY: And we will. And that's wonderful. But what I've been thinking about, too, is all the people we don't know. I mean, every time this happens, there's different women crowded round that mine-head, waiting for word. We've all seen them. Been them.

DOROTHY: Well, what can we do? We can't possibly help everybody.

KAY: Why not? *(Beat.)* I know. It's absolutely pie-in-the-sky but...but if we could, how on earth would we go about it?

DOROTHY: Well, organize, I guess.

KAY: Organize? A union? This is Dorothy talking?

DOROTHY:    No, I don't mean union, I mean organize something like a ladies aid group or I don't know...

KAY:    A Ladies Auxiliary. You are absolutely right. I remember Bob saying some of the locals south of the border have auxiliaries. Well, that's what we need here. We need to set up a Ladies Auxiliary to the main union.

DOROTHY:    Well, I'm not so sure it has to be for the...

KAY:    We'll organize a group to support the men and help miners' wives and widows and their kids – help them all back on their feet with a bit of food and friendly support. What's the matter with that?

DOROTHY:    Well, that's kind of like the ladies auxiliary at church, then, in a way.

KAY:    In a way.

DOROTHY:    So, that's...that's probably...

KAY:    Harmless enough? You'll help?

DOROTHY:    Well, I guess I can't see them firing anybody over women holding a few bake sales to help children and such. So, I could probably pitch in with that, sure.

KAY:    Can you type?

DOROTHY:    Why, yes. Yes, I can, actually. My neighbour back in Timmins taught me when Jim was out of work so I could try to find a job – even gave me her old typewriter.

KAY:    Thank God. Because I really don't think you should be in charge of the baking. *(Tapping a rock-hard biscuit.)* Might remind people of the rock bursts.

## Scene 4: WOMEN'S WORK

> *DOROTHY sits down to her typewriter. CÉCILE and POPPY reappear.*

DOROTHY:    *(To audience.)* And so I started typing.

KAY:    Did you ever!

POPPY:    I don't think you ever stopped.

CÉCILE:    You were a marvel. So fast. So accurate.

KAY:    You were a huge support to us.

DOROTHY:    I was only doing it for you, Kay, to support you. I was still no friend of the union. Not then.

KAY:    I know.

DOROTHY:    There was no way I wanted to get Jim in trouble at work, so I just kept telling myself it was only, you know, women's work. Truth be told, though, what you had me typing was sure starting to sound like full-tilt union propaganda...

> *DOROTHY pounds the keys...then pulls the sheet from the typewriter and hands it to KAY... in 1941.*

> *(Images of real-life Ladies Auxiliary promotional pages could be projected.)*

> *While the action below occurs in 1941, the asides to the audience are in the present.*

KAY:    *(Reading the sheet.)* Join the Mine Mill Ladies Auxiliary! We work not only to help one another's families, but to help the Mine Mill Union...help us improve general conditions by increasing wages and shortening hours of labour...and improve working conditions by removing or preventing the dangers – eliminating the dust, smoke, and poisonous fumes and improving ventilation and lighting! *(Marvelling.)* I can't believe it. Not a single typo.

*KAY takes it & heads off to canvass.*

DOROTHY:    *(To audience.)* Kay would get the pages mimeographed and go door to door with them. Of course, she started with women she knew, where there'd be more chance of a warm welcome.

*KAY knocks and POPPY answers.*

POPPY:    Of course, you can count me in. After all the casseroles and clothes you've given us? Besides, Danny says Florence Nightingale I'm not, so I've gotta be useful some other way. What can I do?

*POPPY takes the sheet and knocks on another doorstep. (Perhaps with a "Shave and a Haircut" knock that CÉCILE recognizes.) CÉCILE answers eagerly – then looks carefully at the paper POPPY holds.*

CÉCILE:    *Ah, ma chouette. Je ne sais pas.* The company won't like this at all, *non, non, non.* And do we need another union?

POPPY:    Another union?

CÉCILE:        *Mon* Alphonse, he said the company is starting its own union, *hein?* That will protect the workers better than strangers from outside.

POPPY:         Company union? That's a laugh. Nah, they're just afraid of us. We need a real union to work for real change.

CÉCILE:        But what kind of change could we –

POPPY:         Safer working conditions! Compensation they can't yank away from us just like that. And isn't it high time the men got down to a forty-eight-hour work week?

CÉCILE:        Forty-eight hours, *Mon Dieu.* We can't get too pie-in-the-sky now. That would be like a holiday *à la plage, hein?* Maybe that's to tempt us. The priest says the Mine Mill union is run by communists.

POPPY:         Do I look red to you? Apart from my fingernails! Or are you worried they'll make Alphonse start dancing like a Cossack if he joins?

CÉCILE:        Might be worth helping you, just to see that.

POPPY:         Talk to Alphonse. Kay's husband Bob has the union cards...

DOROTHY:       *(To audience.)* So sometimes the door-to-door leafletting went pretty well. Other times...

               *KAY becomes a policeman.*

KAY as
POLICEMAN:     You! You there! May I ask you what you think you're doing?

POPPY:         Well, officer, I'm...er...visiting – a friend.

KAY as
POLICEMAN:     And who might that be?

POPPY:            Mrs...uh...*(Peeking at her list.)* Bernardi!

KAY as
POLICEMAN:        I know the Bernardis. So you're looking for
                  Leone's wife, Rina?

POPPY:            Rina! Right! Rina and I, we're – like that.

                  *She crosses her fingers.*

KAY as
POLICEMAN:        Really. And what's that you've got there?

POPPY:            A recipe for...perogies.

KAY as
POLICEMAN:        Is that right? Thing is, if you really knew Rina
                  Bernardi, you'd know she'd never want a
                  recipe for any "perogies." You'd also know
                  she's been gone since before the war. Took
                  little Mario and the other kids back to Italy – to
                  learn Italian, Dante, classical music, the whole
                  bit. And you'd know Rina probably won't be
                  back until little Mario Bernardi is well on his
                  way to being some kind of famous conductor or
                  something. So you'd know there's no reason to
                  be on her doorstep today with this...*(Grabbing
                  the leaflet.)* This recipe for "perogies" which
                  sure looks like unsolicited union propaganda
                  to me. *(They stare at each other.)* Which means
                  we have a date downtown, young lady.

POPPY:            A date?

KAY as
POLICEMAN:        Yes, I'm taking you downtown. Come on now.

POPPY:            Sir, I'm flattered, I am. But you've got the wrong
                  idea. I'm a married woman.

KAY as
POLICEMAN:   Why, I didn't mean...

*POPPY laughs.*

Oh, you know perfectly well what I mean – I mean, to the police station! Right now!

POPPY:   *(To audience.)* And that was it: I was arrested. They offered me a phone call when I got down there, like they do. But we didn't have a phone, so, after a while, they just let me go.

KAY as
POLICEMAN:   Now, I'm sure this is just a case of a little lady getting mixed up in things beyond her scope, but let this be a warning to you.

POPPY:   Oh, yes, officer. I consider myself warned.

*(To the audience.)* To carry a few recipes with me the next time I go leafletting!

*They all stay in the present now.*

CÉCILE:   Poppy! You make it sound like so much fun. Like getting arrested was all laughing all over the place. But you were scared, I remember. When you were waiting and waiting there at the police...you were trembling. You told me.

POPPY:   Did I? That's not how I remember it now.

CÉCILE:   No, back in Forty-One, we were all still so scared and it was all still in secret, *hein?* Pretending to bring recipes, like that.

KAY:   Taking care not to say the wrong thing to the wrong person.

DOROTHY:   Pamphlets and union cards passed hand to hand, tucked into pockets, hidden away if anyone looked.

CÉCILE:         That's how it was.

DOROTHY:        An underground movement. Fitting for a mining community.

## Scene 5: UNDERGROUND MOVEMENT

> *A shift into the past once again.*

> *The women put on miners' helmets and become their husbands back in 1941. They have more than a bit of fun with their imitations…*

> *CÉCILE once again becomes ALPHONSE, holding a union card:*

**CÉCILE
as ALPHONSE:** The union? *Oui, bien sûr.* Count me in. I'm not afraid no more. It's time, *hein?* Time to stand together. Hey, maybe I'll be so busy with the union, I'll have no time to go to church.

> *He kisses his union card.*

> *DOROTHY is now JIM.*

**DOROTHY
as JIM:** Dammit, Al! Get that out of sight! My wife catches me with one of them union cards and she'll beat me black and blue. (*Smacks his fist.*) Besides, I've got myself a job and I want to keep it that way. There's not a snowball's chance in hell the company's going to recognize the union and you know it.

> *KAY is now BOB. (As BOB speaks, ALPHONSE may throw in an enthusiastic "Oui" and "Bien sûr!")*

**KAY
as BOB:** Aw, it's just a matter of time, Jim. How long can they hold out when we all stand up to them, every last one of us? We stand together, refuse to flinch and let the company start to tremble! So, how about some liquid courage to steel our nerves? Let's all us boys head down to the Ashcan for a pint and a game or two – dealer's choice!

*POPPY is now DANNY.*

POPPY
as DANNY:      You said it, Bob! I'm in. For that and one of these
               union cards – *(Takes a union card.)* After all, did
               I ever tell you about my days in Estevan?

KAY
as BOB:        Only about a hundred –

POPPY
as DANNY:      *(Not to be interrupted.)* Coal miner riots of
               Thirty-One. They couldn't stop me there and
               they're not going to stop me here. I may be a
               half-crippled-up son of a bitch now but I got
               time on my hands – or, thanks to the gimpy
               arm, the one hand anyway – so I'm gonna put
               it to good use. So, yeah, I'm standing by the
               union. Along with my wife. A true Union Maid.

               *Still as the men, they launch into a rousing union
               song, preferably Woody Guthrie's "Union Maid."
               (See lyrics in script below.)*

               *(Note: As of 2018, "Union Maid" entered the
               public domain and became free for use in Canada.
               For performances in the U.S. and elsewhere
               outside Canada, the theatre may require a
               performance licence. Other public domain song
               options do exist, however. Contact the playwright
               for other suggestions.)*

               *While BOB, DANNY, and ALPHONSE begin the
               song, at some point JIM is pulled into the song
               against his better judgment.*

ALL:           "THERE ONCE WAS A UNION MAID, SHE NEVER
                   WAS AFRAID
               OF GOONS AND GINKS AND COMPANY FINKS
               AND THE DEPUTY SHERIFFS WHO MADE THE RAID.

SHE WENT TO THE UNION HALL, WHEN A
    MEETING IT WAS CALLED,
AND WHEN THE LEGION BOYS COME 'ROUND
SHE ALWAYS STOOD HER GROUND.

*(Chorus:)*

OH, YOU CAN'T SCARE ME, I'M STICKING TO
    THE UNION,
I'M STICKING TO THE UNION, I'M STICKING TO
    THE UNION.
OH, YOU CAN'T SCARE ME, I'M STICKING TO THE
    UNION,
I'M STICKING TO THE UNION 'TIL THE DAY I DIE."

"THIS UNION MAID WAS WISE, TO THE TRICKS OF
    COMPANY SPIES,
SHE COULDN'T BE FOOLED BY A COMPANY
    STOOL, SHE'D ALWAYS ORGANIZE THE GUYS.
SHE ALWAYS GOT HER WAY, WHEN SHE STRUCK
    FOR BETTER PAY.
SHE'D SHOW HER CARD TO THE NATIONAL
    GUARD
AND THIS IS WHAT SHE'D SAY:

*(Chorus:)*

OH, YOU CAN'T SCARE ME, I'M STICKING TO
    THE UNION,
I'M STICKING TO THE UNION, I'M STICKING TO
    THE UNION.
OH, YOU CAN'T SCARE ME, I'M STICKING TO THE
    UNION,
I'M STICKING TO THE UNION 'TIL THE DAY I DIE."

*They attack the song with an almost giddy sense of*
*fun, at some point, turning into themselves as the*
*women again, and back into the present.*

KAY:            It did feel like that sometimes, didn't it? Giddy,
                almost.

POPPY:          Absolutely!

DOROTHY:        There were the highs, no question, when we
                were really flying.

CÉCILE:         But there were also the lows.

KAY:            When the company played dirty.

POPPY:          Real dirty.

## Scene 6: UNION MAID

> *DOROTHY is typing furiously when KAY arrives. KAY is obviously shaken.*

DOROTHY: Kay! What's the matter?

> *KAY can't speak.*

Oh no. Has there been – is Bob okay?

> *KAY shakes her head.*

KAY: No. No, he's not.

DOROTHY: Oh no. Oh dear Lord.

KAY: No, no. Not that. No, Bob's alive. He's not been hurt.

DOROTHY: Thank God.

KAY: You're right, it could be so much worse. It could. It's just – they fired him.

DOROTHY: No.

KAY: Found out he'd been organizing for the union.

DOROTHY: Kay, I'm so sorry.

KAY: After everything he's done for that company. Twelve-and-a-half years. Someone didn't show for a shift – there was Bob. He filled it. Even on Christmas. He gave up his Christmas dinner just last year. For them. Well, I guess this is how they show their appreciation. You knew it would come to this. You'll say we should have known.

DOROTHY: No, Kay. I did worry, but that's not…

KAY: There's no money, of course. We've been buying groceries on credit like everybody else. I don't know where the money goes, it just goes.

DOROTHY: A man like Bob'll get work. At one of the other mines.

KAY: Not when the bosses spread word about him being a union man. And worse than that. Wasn't just him today. Down at one of the other levels, someone lost his union card. Fell out of his pocket or something. But there was no name on the card – he hadn't signed it yet – so, they went and fired every man working on that level.

DOROTHY: Oh no.

KAY: Every one of them. That's more than a hundred men lost their jobs today. One day.

DOROTHY: Dear Lord.

KAY: Where's Jim?

DOROTHY: No, no, Jim's all right. He only just left to start his shift. But you're right. He could have lost his job today too, along with all the rest of them. *(Beat.)* Kay, what can I do?

KAY: I don't know, teach me how many times you can boil the same soup bone? You've had your share of tough times.

DOROTHY: No, Kay, what can I do for the union – for the Ladies Auxiliary. Officially. This isn't right. None of this is right. They think they can divide and conquer us. Well, what happens if everybody joins? Even people like me and Jim. I mean, they can't fire everybody, can they now?

KAY: What's got into you?

DOROTHY:      Sense, I think.

KAY:          A true Union Maid, who never was afraid.

DOROTHY:      Oh, she's still afraid. She's just joining the fight anyway.

## Scene 7: PRESSURE BUILDING

> *CÉCILE and POPPY rejoin DOROTHY and KAY in the present.*

POPPY:          And, woo! Once you joined!

KAY:            There was no stopping you.

CÉCILE:         You put us all to shame.

DOROTHY:        Well, that's just not true. But I did end up knocking on so many doors, my knuckles were raw meat.

POPPY:          The only meat any of us saw that winter!

KAY:            Did you ever bring them in.

DOROTHY:        If a man hadn't joined already, the wife talked 'em into it.

POPPY:          You think it was the talking that did it? I know a few gals who said it took more than that!

> *CÉCILE stifles a laugh.*

KAY:            However we did it, suddenly almost everyone was behind the union at last. Local 240 was the talk of the town.

> *Through the next section, the women turn the sheets into small tents.*
>
> *They talk to the audience and each other as they work, their indignation rising with the tents…*

DOROTHY:        With the whole community onside, you'd think the companies would finally have listened to reason.

POPPY:          You would, wouldja?

KAY:            Instead, they just…ignored us.

CÉCILE:    There was no law then said a company had to bargain with a union.

DOROTHY:    So the company just kept on doing what it was doing.

POPPY:    Paying starvation wages for death-defying work.

KAY:    Fifty-seven cents an hour. Same wage they'd had for ten years.

POPPY:    And before you go thinking that must have been something back in those days, lemme tell you it wasn't.

KAY:    With a war on, inflation was bad.

CÉCILE:    The price of food and rent, it kept going up and up and up.

DOROTHY:    And everything already cost more in mining towns like Kirkland Lake.

POPPY:    Where they know they've got ya!

KAY:    All of us knew how to stretch a dollar from here to Sudbury but things were getting outrageous.

CÉCILE:    There is nothing on this earth harder than a little one, pulling at your leg, saying, "I'm hungry."

DOROTHY:    And that was our life. Life in Kirkland Lake.

POPPY:    We haven't even told them about how the men had to buy their jobs in the first place.

KAY:    Job selling. Don't get me started!

DOROTHY:    You know, I'd forgotten about that. But that's how Jim got his job.

POPPY:    That's how most of the men got on at the mines.

*trapped for low wages*

CÉCILE:        You pay the mine boss to get the job, *hein?* Pay it off over time.

DOROTHY:       That's right. You had to promise a kickback to the mine boss – and pay him every payday until the price for the job was met.

POPPY:         But once a job was paid off, weren't the bosses good at finding reasons to fire a man – so they could sell that job all over again and keep the kickbacks coming!

CÉCILE:        It was wrong, but that's how it was, *hein?*

KAY:           Basically, the companies owned you. They owned everything. Even the newspapers.

POPPY:         No!        *power / control*

KAY:           Bill Wright of the Wright-Hargreaves Mine?

DOROTHY:       He owned the *Globe and Mail.*

POPPY:         No wonder they didn't print my letter to the editor.

CÉCILE:        Could also have been the four-letter words, Poppy.

KAY:           Thing is, it's bad enough to be owned, period. But when the owners start thinking they can get away with anything?

               *She shakes her head.*

POPPY:         What we're saying is…things were bad.

KAY:           And getting worse.

DOROTHY:       A lot worse.

POPPY:         'Til there was no other choice.

KAY:           We'd tried everything else.

| | |
|---|---|
| CÉCILE: | *C'est vrai.* We were forced into it. |
| DOROTHY: | No one wants a strike – ever. |
| POPPY: | Nobody. |
| KAY: | All the same, that winter, the men at all eight gold mines in Kirkland Lake went out on strike. Together. |
| DOROTHY: | Nearly four thousand men. |
| POPPY: | And we women were behind them all the way. |
| CÉCILE: | It was peaceful too, they should know that. |
| KAY: | The men kept it orderly. Civil. We were all proud of that. |
| DOROTHY: | The picket line stretched all along the main street. "The Mile of Gold" they called it. |
| POPPY: | That's because seven of the gold mines were right along that street. |
| CÉCILE: | *Non, non.* They called it that because the street was paved with gold. |
| DOROTHY: | What? |
| KAY: | Story goes that the construction crew that built the road, way back when, accidentally took rock from an ore storage pile. |
| POPPY: | Get out of here! |
| CÉCILE: | By the time they figure it out, it was all covered with concrete. Would have cost too much to dig it all up again so they leave it like that. |
| DOROTHY: | Well, along that "Mile of Gold" they set up little tents where the men on strike could go to try to warm up. Kind of like these. |

*They survey the tents they've made. (They glow, possibly lit from inside with battery-powered votive candles.)*

KAY:        They don't look quite right, do they? What have we done wrong?

POPPY:      Ah, they're close enough. Let 'em use their imagination.

            *(To the audience.)* They're tents.

DOROTHY:    They sure needed the tents, too. What a winter.

CÉCILE:     Winter of '41–'42.

KAY:        Bitter, bitter cold.

POPPY:      That's right. The strike didn't start 'til –

KAY:        November 18th. That's when they went out.

            *The women don winter coats and pick up thermoses to move into the next scene.*

POPPY:      Wait.

            *POPPY takes down one of the sheets, balls it up and stuffs it under her coat to become visibly pregnant.*

            There. That's more like it. *(After picking up a thermos.)* HOT COFFEE COMIN' THROUGH! WOO!!

            *POPPY exits.*

DOROTHY:    Will we really have to shout out? In front of all those men on the picket line?

KAY:        I don't know, hollering at 'em might be fun. *(Trying it out.)* HEY FELLAS, GET YOUR BUTTS OVER HERE – NOW! AND I MEAN NOW!! *(A moment, then:)* You know, Dorothy, you should give that a try. You might just like it.

## Scene 8: FIRST FALTERING STEPS

*A shift to later that night – the wee hours. KAY, CÉCILE, and DOROTHY are on the street with empty thermoses.*

*We hear the sound of a truck stopping, then the door opening and slamming shut. POPPY appears.*

POPPY:        Hey! Over here! Before you refill your thermoses, come warm up in the truck.

CÉCILE:       We won't all fit.

POPPY:        Sure we will. Cuddle in and get cozy, girls!

KAY:          Oh, twist our rubber arms!

*They seat themselves side by side as if squished into the front of a truck. They shiver, blow on their fingers.*

Bitter, bitter night.

POPPY:        How's it going out there?

DOROTHY:      Better than I thought it would. I'm actually starting to like walking that picket line.

CÉCILE:       The men are so…appreciative. That's the word, *hein?*

DOROTHY:      It is. The perfect word.

*CÉCILE is pleased.*

KAY:          Well, I'm clearly not doing as well as you two. My fingers are so numb here I go and fumble the coffee – spill it all over that one little fella. Greasy little guy. I forget his name.

DOROTHY:      Greasy?

KAY:       Oh, you've seen him. Slicks his hair back with so much homemade lard, he smells like a pound of bacon. Old bacon.

POPPY:     You mean Maurice!

KAY:       That's it! Well, didn't I soak his coat clear through. Is he mad.

DOROTHY:   Now, there's one way to warm the men up. Dump the coffee right on them!

CÉCILE:    All well and good – till it freezes.

*They laugh.*

POPPY:     Maurice had it coming.

DOROTHY:   Why do you say that?

POPPY:     Man like that always has it coming. The look on his face.

CÉCILE:    Poppy.

POPPY:     No, I mean it. The way he leers at ya. Not to mention those wandering hands of his. I don't know what my friend Eva sees in him. I've warned her. He's nothing but a bully. And a mean drunk. Just ask the fellas. And when a man's like that with the fellas, it's only a matter of time before he's like that with his girl. If he hasn't started smacking her around already.

*Beat.*

DOROTHY:   We should get back out there.

KAY:       Hey, but what's the latest on your friend's husband? The one who's overseas, flying Spitfires. I thought I'd read he'd gone missing. At least if I'm remembering the name right. It's Wally, isn't it? Wally Floody?

DOROTHY:      He got shot down over France last month but they finally got word. He's alive, but they've got him in a German P.O.W. camp.

CÉCILE:       *Mon Dieu.*

DOROTHY·      Betty's at her wit's end.

POPPY:        But he's a miner? From here?

DOROTHY:      Yeah.

POPPY:        No way a Kirkland Lake miner's going to stay stuck in a camp like that for long. Our boys can tunnel their way out of anything.

DOROTHY:      That's what I said! I wrote her and said, "Mark my words, Wally's going to make some kind of great escape, just you wait and see."

CÉCILE:       Great Escape. I like that. I'll pray for that, for sure.

POPPY:        Well, gals, this has been swell but...

KAY:          Yep. We should get back out there.

CÉCILE:       *(To DOROTHY.)* Maybe we should start at the other end this time, *hein?*

DOROTHY:      Good idea. *(To the others.)* Going the other way, we nearly didn't have enough coffee left for all the young fellas way out there at the end of the line.

KAY:          Young fellas?

DOROTHY:      Maybe they got missed on the other shifts. Because weren't they just thrilled when we showed up.

CÉCILE:       *Oui!* Kept thanking and thanking us. Lovely boys.

KAY:        Wait, you don't mean down at the far, far end of the line? Past all the strike tents?

DOROTHY:    Yes, right by the gates there. We almost didn't see them at first.

CÉCILE:     But when we did, we hurry right over there and they are so happy. Drank it up like they never see hot coffee before.

DOROTHY:    They even said they'd be sure to tell the union what a good job we were doing.

            *POPPY and KAY start to laugh.*

            What is it?

KAY:        Those weren't strikers.

CÉCILE:     What do you mean?

POPPY:      You were down there bringing comfort and coffee…to the scabs!!

DOROTHY:    What?! No!

CÉCILE:     *Non!*

POPPY:      Yep. And I hate to tell you this, Cécile, but I'll bet they're the ones I saw dropped off by a certain Catholic priest you know.

CÉCILE:     *Non!*

POPPY:      Yep. He drove some of them down there in his truck. The scab workers. Came out from under a tarp.

CÉCILE:     I don't believe it.

POPPY:      The fellas say he's even been writing notes for some of them, telling the company what good workers they'll be, how loyal.

| | |
|---|---|
| CÉCILE: | Our priest? From *L'Assomption?* |
| POPPY: | *Oui!* Sorry. Anyway, the scabs are doing well enough for tonight, don't you think? After free lifts from the priest and free coffee from Cécile and Dorothy. |
| DOROTHY: | Oh, please don't say that. |
| POPPY: | Might as well laugh about it. And here some of the men wondered how helpful the Auxiliary would be. But, never fear, here we are, bringing comfort to the cowards! |
| KAY: | Strength to the strikebreakers! |
| POPPY: | Solace to all the sons of bitches! |
| DOROTHY: | Oh, please stop. |
| POPPY: | Angels of mercy to the assh – |
| CÉCILE: | Poppy, *non!* |
| DOROTHY: | I can't believe we… |
| CÉCILE: | They were so happy. |
| DOROTHY: | I'm so sorry. |
| KAY: | So what? We'll get better at this. |
| CÉCILE: | Truly, we can't get any worse. |

*The women laugh as they shift back into the present…which is warmer.*

## Scene 9: INTO LOCK STEP

> *The women take off their coats and talk as they set up what they'll need for the Ladies Auxiliary meeting they're heading into...*

KAY:           We never did let you live that one down, did we?

DOROTHY:       No. You didn't. But then we had it coming.

CÉCILE:        Mistakes can be good. They let the good Lord show us how to improve.

POPPY:         One way of looking at it.

KAY:           It's unshakeable, your faith – isn't it, Cécile?

CÉCILE:        *Mon Dieu,* I hope so.

DOROTHY:       Well, your prayers for Wally's "Great Escape" sure helped.

CÉCILE:        They did?

KAY:           They did. Why, in the '60s, they even made a movie about it. *The Great Escape* with Wally the "Tunnel King" played by Charles Bronson, no less.

POPPY:         Of course, in the movie, they changed his name and nationality and all but everybody from Kirkland Lake knew it was Wally.

DOROTHY:       But all that was a long while coming. Took us a while too, to get ourselves better organized.

KAY:           Not that long! You had us working with military precision by Christmas.

CÉCILE:        Even before then. You had us very serious, very organized by the seventh of December.

POPPY:         The seventh? How can you possibly remember the day?

CÉCILE:        Pearl Harbour.

               *CÉCILE crosses herself.*

POPPY:         That's right. Everything got so urgent.

DOROTHY:       What a time that was. *(Remembering.)* Yeah,
               we were busy with the war effort, on top of
               everything else.

KAY:           We sure were – war bond drives, knitting for
               the troops overseas.

CÉCILE:        Getting all the children out collecting scrap
               metal for recycling, remember?

POPPY:         And in the midst of all that, there you were,
               Dorothy – absolutely hell-bent on getting us
               Mine Mill ladies into lock step.

DOROTHY:       Oh, it wasn't just my doing. It was group effort
               – it took every one of us, working together.

KAY:           But, it's true, right from that first meeting you
               chaired, you were becoming quite the drill
               sergeant.

DOROTHY:       Well, I don't know if –

               *A teasing look from KAY.*

               Then again, maybe I was.

               *DOROTHY pounds at the typewriter keys again,
               creating the sound of rhythmic march with the
               keys and the carriage bell.*

               *The women march in step...right into a meeting
               room for a Ladies Auxiliary meeting.*

               Ten-hut!

               *The women stand to attention.*

POPPY:    Reporting for duty with the Mine Mill Ladies Auxiliary, sir!

KAY:    All present and accounted for, sir!

CÉCILE:    Coffee, tea, and Nanaimo bars on the side table, sir!

POPPY:    Ooh, yummy!

DOROTHY:    At ease, ladies.

    *The dive into the treats. We hear the sound of a modest crowd.*

    All right, ladies. Order, order. First on the agenda, our membership update. Kay?

KAY:    Right. As agreed at the last meeting, we have set our auxiliary dues at fifty cents a month. Please don't leave without getting your booklet stamped, ladies – it'll show you're paid up. Also, please speak to me privately if the fifty cents would cause hardship – arrangements can be made.

DOROTHY:    Thank you, Kay. Next, we need to finalize our program of work for the coming year. I hope you've all carefully reviewed the list we made last time – kindly circulated by Cécile's youngest the other day. Please thank her for us, Cécile.

CÉCILE:    I will. *Merci.*

POPPY:    Josephine's turning ten soon, isn't she?

CÉCILE:    *Oui.*

KAY:    She's such a little doll.

DOROTHY:    Ladies, please. We have a long agenda to get through.

KAY:            Aren't you all business all of a sudden!

DOROTHY:        You asked me to chair the meeting, so that's what I'm –

KAY:            No, no, you're right. Go on.

DOROTHY:        Is there any final discussion on our program?

                *They become some other women at the meeting. MILLIE raises her hand.*

                Millie? Go ahead.

POPPY
as MILLIE:      I still think number one should be "support of our parent organization" – the Mine Mill union. That comes above all.

DOROTHY:        Excellent point. Thank you, Millie. Any further discussion on that? Yes, Bernice.

CÉCILE
as BERNICE:     That's all well and good but I was thinking we need something practical on there about ways to raise funds for strike support.

DOROTHY
as ILA:         No doubt about that. Our emergency fund is pretty near cleaned out. That's a fact. That's all I've got to say.

KAY
as VELMA:       First things first, Ila! We need the union to force men to babysit so we can even get to these meetings. I almost didn't make it here tonight and that's why, and I'm not happy about it!

DOROTHY:        Velma, Ila, please. There's too many of us here to jump in like that. Please remember to raise your hands. Now, where were we?

                *(Seeing Poppy's hand.)* Poppy.

POPPY:          For fundraising, I figure a Hard Times Dance might be fun. Complete with Lindy Hop contest.

CÉCILE:         You can do the Lindy Hop?

POPPY:          You betcha! Me and Danny have been practising ever since we saw *Hellzapoppin!* Wanna see?

                *POPPY starts to get up to demonstrate.*

KAY:            You can get Danny to dance?

DOROTHY:        Ladies. Please. We're getting off track here. Not to be a stickler, but I see fundraisers not as separate program items – more as part of number one: support of parent organization. The particulars we can discuss at a later date.

CÉCILE:         *Oui,* that makes sense.

POPPY:          Hell, I don't care how you list it. I just want a dance.

DOROTHY:        So, our final list now includes:

POPPY
as MILLIE:      Support of parent organization,

CÉCILE
as BERNICE:     Lobbying for price control,

DOROTHY
as ILA:         Setting up a political action committee,

KAY
as VELMA:       Improving our organization overall, including childcare!

CÉCILE:         Childcare, *oui!* And teenage problems,

POPPY:          Health, housing,

CÉCILE:        Community work,

POPPY:         And racial injustice.

DOROTHY:       Have we got everything?

KAY:           Oh, number twelve: "World Peace."

               *(The actual handwritten copy of this very real Ladies Auxiliary "To Do" list could be projected here.)*

DOROTHY:       Right. World Peace.

               *(To audience.)* To say we were ambitious doesn't begin to cover it.

               *They all shift into the present.*

KAY:           It wasn't all talk, either.

POPPY:         No way.

CÉCILE:        *Pas du tout.* We made things happen.

POPPY:         Like with the donations. Dorothy would pound out appeals for help, all of us would pound the pavement, and even though I thought I might have to start pounding some heads, sure enough, the help came rolling in.

               *A shift back into another Ladies Auxiliary meeting in late 1941...*

KAY:           *(Opening an envelope.)* Look at this – from the Glace Bay miners, all the way out in Nova Scotia. We're getting money from across Canada now.

DOROTHY:       And from union locals right across the United States. *(Waving another envelope.)* Arizona!

CÉCILE:        And food, from all around.

*The women might hand a large basket from one to another as if in a sandbag line – or perhaps mime this action.*

KAY:            Potatoes from Temagami!

CÉCILE:         Beans from *la belle province!*

POPPY:          Carrots from Cobalt!

KAY:            And cod liver oil!

                *POPPY grimaces.*

CÉCILE:         Children need their milk and cod liver oil, *hein?*

                *The basket is suddenly so heavy it hits the floor.*

DOROTHY:        Hey, Christmas cake! From Timmins.

KAY:            A ton of it too.

POPPY:          It literally looks like one ton of Christmas cake.

CÉCILE:         They must like their Christmas cake in Timmins.

POPPY:          Or not.

DOROTHY:        Look at all the clothes. Coats, hats, mitts.

CÉCILE:         And toys! For Christmas! So *Père Noël* can come after all.

                *One or more may hum a bar or two of "O Christmas Tree."*

KAY:            The woodcutting crews are sure working out great.

POPPY:          Men cut the wood. Kids divvy it up. Every family gets their fair share.

DOROTHY:        Wasn't that your idea, Cécile? Genius!

CÉCILE: *Merci. (Catching herself.)* Of course, all good ideas come from the good Lord above. *(Beat.)* But it's something, *hein?* What we're doing here. Fuel for the wood stoves, food for the stomachs. All so no one will be hungry or cold. Or at least not *too* hungry or *too* cold.

*A shift back into the present...*

*They may start putting on their coats to leave their meeting...and to enter the next scene.*

KAY: We did that.

DOROTHY: All of that.

CÉCILE: It was a lot, *hein?*

POPPY: No kidding. I'm starting to think we were bloody amazing.

KAY: A force to be reckoned with.

DOROTHY: Well, with all the support we were giving the men, it's no wonder the strike was holding firm.

KAY: So I guess it's also no wonder the government decided to send in the troops – literally.

*The sound of an army marching...*

CÉCILE: We heard them before we saw them.

DOROTHY: An army of provincial police.

POPPY: Courtesy of Premier Mitch Hepburn.

KAY: So we called 'em Hepburn's Hussars.

POPPY: I called 'em Sons of Mitch's!

DOROTHY: But most of us called them...

ALL: Terrifying.

## Scene 10: HEPBURN'S HUSSARS

> *1941. An army of provincial police bears down on the women.*
>
> *(Archival photos of the marching police could be projected.)*

CÉCILE:     Let's get out of the way, *hein? Allons-y!*

POPPY:      They can't do this!

DOROTHY:    They *are* doing this.

KAY:        Let's get out of here now.

POPPY:      They want to clear out the strikers? Well, technically we're not the ones on strike, are we, now, so – hey! Watch where you're going, buddy! Hey!

> *The women are jostled back.*

CÉCILE:     Poppy! *Fais attention!*

KAY:        She's right, Poppy. Stay back. Well back.

DOROTHY:    They clearly don't care who's in their way.

CÉCILE:     But a young mother-to-be? *Mon Dieu.*

POPPY:      There's an inspector! He should know what they're doing to citizens walking on town roads – public roads.

KAY:        I'm not sure he's going to care.

POPPY:      But they're public roads! And I'm the public!

CÉCILE:     Poppy.

> *DOROTHY becomes the POLICE INSPECTOR. She speaks into a megaphone.*

DOROTHY
as INSPECTOR: Tear down those tents and clear the street. Clear the street immediately – or face the consequences.

KAY:  I don't like the sound of that.

CÉCILE:  *Non, moi non plus.*

DOROTHY
as INSPECTOR: I repeat. All tents are to be torn down and all are to clear the street. Immediately. This is your final warning.

> *The women step back as we hear the sound of smashing glass and ripping fabric. Their tents start to fall.*

POPPY:  I can't believe they're…

DOROTHY:  They won't pull that one down. Not in a million years. That one's flying the Union Jack.

KAY:  You're right. Not with them flying the flag. And with the portrait of the King and Queen up like that. They'd never –

> *They watch in horror as even that tent is torn down.*

POPPY:  Okay, that's it. I'm going over there.

CÉCILE:  *Non, non, non, non, NON!*

> *CÉCILE grabs POPPY with surprising force. The women watch the provincial police as they march past them in a final show of force. There is a brief silence before…*

KAY:  I never dreamed I'd see this, in my own country.

CÉCILE:  A public street. In broad daylight.

DOROTHY:  This, we remember. All of us.

KAY:          Kirkland Lake, Ontario.

CÉCILE:       In this day and age, 1941.

DOROTHY:      In Canada. A free country.

POPPY:        Think of what our boys are fighting for,
              overseas, right this minute. But here at home?
              We're not allowed to stand up for workers'
              rights here at home in our free country.

              *DOROTHY is at one of the fallen tents, picking
              things up slowly, in shock.*

CÉCILE:       Come on now. We need to get inside and get
              warm. Especially you, Poppy. *Allons-y.*

              *The women turn to leave, except for DOROTHY,
              who is crouched by one of the fallen tents. KAY
              goes to her.*

KAY:          Dorothy?

              *DOROTHY pulls out a trampled Union Jack and
              a portrait of the King and Queen...the glass is
              broken.*

DOROTHY:      I can't...it doesn't...

KAY:          Make sense?

              *DOROTHY shakes her head.*

              No. Of course it doesn't.

DOROTHY:      When they marched past us, I wanted to shout
              at them, stop them somehow. I mean, I'm not
              expecting, like Poppy. I could have run up and
              told them off, every one of them. Why didn't I
              speak up? Step up? What on earth is the matter
              with me?

KAY:          Why, there's nothing the – Dorothy, you're
              shocked is all. Of course you are. We all are. But
              we can't let this –

DOROTHY:    No, I mean it. Why do the words fail me? Right when I need them most. I can say them to all of you. I can type them. I can think them. Why can't I say something when it counts? In front of the men in charge.

KAY:    Push come to shove, maybe you're not just a woman of words, you're a woman of action.

*A shift back into the present. CÉCILE, POPPY, and KAY could start turning the fallen tents back into hanging sheets.*

DOROTHY:    You did it there too. I honestly can't count the number of times you did.

KAY:    What?

DOROTHY:    Change my life.

KAY:    Oh, for Heaven's sakes. You're getting dramatic on us.

DOROTHY:    No, I'm not. It was like a road opened up right in front of me. And you opened it – or made me see it somehow. This gleaming grand avenue. Our road ahead: the real mile of gold.

KAY:    Go on with you.

DOROTHY:    No, it's true. I could suddenly see what we had to do next.

*END OF ACT ONE*

*(Please note: This play can run without an act break but, if one is taken, this is where to do it.)*

# ACT TWO

## Scene 11: WINDS OF CHANGE

> *1941, back in their meeting room.*
>
> *DOROTHY unfurls a large banner – perhaps one of the sheets – with the words "You Can't Scare Us WE'RE STICKING TO OUR UNION" perhaps printed or projected on it.*
>
> *(Note: This banner is clearly seen in one of the archival photographs from the day of the march. That photograph might be projected here, if projections are used.)*

DOROTHY: And...*voilà! (Reading out banner.)* "You can't scare us. We're sticking to our union." What do you think, ladies?

POPPY: Hunky-dory in my books!

KAY: You've nailed the sentiment, that's for sure.

CÉCILE: You've sewn it up so nicely but...I don't know. That won't work so well as a flag, I don't think. It would take a big wind to get that flying.

POPPY: Or a lot of hot air. Luckily the company men will have that covered.

KAY: No, she means to set it up, like the strikers do out on the line with their signs. Don't you, Dorothy?

DOROTHY: Actually...

POPPY:        What's the point? With those marching Sons of Mitch's all around the town, that sign'll last about two whole minutes.

DOROTHY:      No, I don't mean just set it up. I mean, march with it.

KAY:          March?

DOROTHY:      It's you who got me thinking about this, Kay. It's time to put our words into action – get 'em moving. You said it yourself, Poppy: they're public roads. This is a free country and we can walk where we like. So we will. We'll gather every woman in this town and we'll march. Together.

CÉCILE:       I don't know. Those police all marching up and down, all around, they're young boys, *oui*? And I know young boys – I raise seven of them. And young boys like that, all dressed up in uniform, they feel like big men. And they do whatever their big bosses tell them – with no thought in their heads. That's what makes them dangerous, *hein*? They don't think – unless you smack them on the head, drag them to church.

POPPY:        I didn't think you'd go to church anymore. Not after your priest helped the scabs.

CÉCILE:       *Mon Dieu!* Of course I still go to church. I go to the *Irish* church. Father Cavanagh, the Irish priest, he didn't forget his flock.

KAY:          Well, we're thrilled to have you all in our parish. *(To the others.)* We're bursting at the seams now. I hear the French church is a cold and empty place these days – except for a few lousy scabs.

CÉCILE:       Don't blame those strikebreakers. They're desperate like us, *hein*? But it was wrong for the priest to sneak them here – and I told him so, God forgive me.

POPPY: I'd like to have seen that.

CÉCILE: *Ouf!* Believe you me, there was nothing to see. I just had a little word with the priest, after mass.

*A shift into that fateful moment...*

*DOROTHY becomes a strict French-Canadian priest. He makes the sign of the cross over CÉCILE.*

I've come for my confession.

DOROTHY
as PRIEST: Once again? But you made your confession before the mass.

CÉCILE: *Non, non.* I've come for the one I need from you. The one I prayed you would give all of us, your faithful parish.

DOROTHY
as PRIEST: *Pardon?*

CÉCILE: I waited, through the mass, to see if you would say something, if you might admit what you did and apologize. I was ready to forgive you if you had.

DOROTHY
as PRIEST: You? Forgive me?

CÉCILE: Alphonse and my boys work so hard in the mine. The work breaks their bones. Sometimes their spirit. So always we come to the Church. I bring them. To the Church. To keep us strong. And now the strike tries to break us too, but still we stay strong, still we struggle together, still we come to the Church. We come to you. Only to find, *Mon Père,* that you have forsaken us. When you go behind our backs, bring strikebreakers to the mine, you don't break the strike, *non.* And you don't break us. You break our trust in you.

*CÉCILE turns to leave.*

DOROTHY
as PRIEST:     You turn your back on the Church?

CÉCILE:     Oh, *non, non.* I turn my back on you. You are not the Church.

*The PRIEST is speechless.*

*CÉCILE returns to the women in the present.*

*Through what follows, they may begin to put on their coats, preparing to leave the meeting.*

Ah, *non, non*, there was nothing to see. I just explained why I had to go. Then I went straight to your church, Kay.

KAY:     You never saw someone run to the confessional so fast.

POPPY:     Well, good for you, is all I say.

DOROTHY:     Listen, if you can stand up to your priest, Cécile, and even switch churches, we can all stand up to Hepburn's Hussars. We can show them what a march through town really looks like.

POPPY:     If there were enough of us, maybe.

KAY:     There'd have to be enough.

CÉCILE:     How would we gather enough women, anyway? With so much to do – and children to care for?

POPPY:     The kids could come too. That would sure boost our numbers.

KAY:     They'd never hurt us then.

POPPY:     They wouldn't dare.

CÉCILE:     It would be okay for the older ones, maybe, but not *les bébés*.

DOROTHY:    We'd ask the men to babysit the wee ones. Tell them it's their duty to support us as proud union members. After all, we're doing this to stand up for them.

CÉCILE:     Well…

KAY:        Someone's warming to the idea.

CÉCILE:     It can be good for a man to take care of a baby, now and then.

DOROTHY:    So, you'll do it?

            *They all look to CÉCILE, who takes a moment before answering.*

CÉCILE:     Maybe the winds of change really are blowing. It's cold enough outside for hell to freeze. I'm Irish Catholic now. I'm already standing up for my family. Why not march for them too?

            *DOROTHY hugs CÉCILE.*

## Scene 12: ON THE MARCH

> *The day of the march, late 1941.*
>
> *The winds of change are blowing in hard and cold.*
>
> *Bundled in their coats, they scan the streets for signs of women.*

KAY: Of course, we would have to pick the meanest day of the year.

POPPY: Forty bloody below!

CÉCILE: Don't think about the cold. Think of a roaring fire.

POPPY: Like Hell.

CÉCILE: Poppy!

POPPY: No, I mean, literally like Hell. Here I've been praying the mine bosses will all go to Hell and pronto but, right now, I envy their destination!

CÉCILE: *Mon Dieu.*

DOROTHY: We did say twelve noon, didn't we?

CÉCILE: Well, there's still a few minutes to go.

POPPY: Yeah, but so far there's only two, four... *(Counting silently, then:)* Eighteen. Bloody hell.

DOROTHY: They could be waiting 'til the last minute.

KAY: You'd have to be mad as a March Hare to come out early on a day like this.

POPPY: Or to come at all.

KAY: No, we'll get fifty, sixty women here today. I know it. Remember how keen everyone was at the potluck?

DOROTHY:   Oh, they were keen – they just weren't sure how keen their husbands would be to look after the wee ones, remember?

POPPY:   Well, the men are sure as hell going to hear from me at the next union meeting if they don't babysit!

> *They stare off, looking for potential marchers, trying not to think about the cold. And their disappointment.*

DOROTHY:   It's no use. We just didn't get the day for it.

CÉCILE:   Maybe next week…if the weather turns, *hein?*

KAY:   Wait a minute, is that…? No. It's like a snow mirage, my eyes are seeing things now. It's nothing.

CÉCILE:   No, not nothing. I don't think so. Look.

POPPY:   You're right! There's a bunch coming from over there. See them? Woo-hoo! Over here ladies!!

KAY:   No, I was looking over there, see? But there wasn't – oh for Pete's sake. They're coming from there too.

DOROTHY:   And from there – around the corner there. They're coming from –

CÉCILE:   They're coming from everywhere.

> *The wind blows in more women.*

> *(The archival photo of the thousands of women marching in 1941 could be projected onto the sheets.)*

DOROTHY: *(To audience.)* And they kept coming. Women from all across town. Women we knew, who'd already been helping with the Mine Mill Ladies Auxiliary, but the truly shocking thing was all the women we didn't know. Hundreds of women. More than that, even.

POPPY: There's thousands, gotta be. Twenty-five hundred, I betcha. I lost count.

KAY: Nearly three thousand. I'm sure of it.

CÉCILE: *Oui.* With the line stretching back like that. Look – it goes two miles, at least.

KAY: Not too shabby for a town of what? Twenty-one thousand?

POPPY: If that.

> *They link arms and march, straddling both 1941 and the present moment where they talk to the audience.*

DOROTHY: *(To audience.)* And not too shabby for a rather cold winter day.

KAY: Rather cold? Minus forty.

POPPY & KAY: With a wind.

KAY: But how did we feel?

DOROTHY: Overjoyed!

POPPY: Over the bloody moon!

KAY: Elated!

CÉCILE: Our hearts were pounding!

POPPY: You just couldn't see any of that on our faces... because they were all frozen.

*The women turn sharply and trudge into the wind, grimacing. They don't look elated. They trudge...and simply try to breathe through the cold.*

*(The ellipses in the next section mark where we might hear them suck in & exhale sharp, pursed lip breaths; this is "40 below breathing" for those not used to Canadian winters.)*

DOROTHY: We marched down Government Road...and kept on marching. We even marched right past Hepburn's Hussars.

KAY: But they didn't dare stop us. Not this time.

POPPY: They might have if I'd...shouted what I planned to...but I just couldn't. Too...bloody...cold.

KAY: Any words of defiance...literally...froze in our throats.

CÉCILE: No talking...just...keep...marching.

KAY: The further we went, the more women would see us, bundle up, and rush out to join us.

DOROTHY: And the men came too. All those striking miners? They followed in our footsteps.

POPPY: All the men who weren't babysitting!

CÉCILE: We led them all.

DOROTHY: I could hardly believe it. What we were doing.

KAY: The sheer numbers, the sheer force – of us.

POPPY: Every woman in town pulling together, standing up to the companies,

CÉCILE: Standing up for our families,

DOROTHY:       Standing up for ourselves.

KAY:           It felt like we were changing the world.

DOROTHY:       It felt like that – because we were.

POPPY:         We could feel it changing!

CÉCILE:        Right in our bones.

POPPY (or ALL): WOO HOO!

> *They stand in their moment of triumph for several more seconds, relishing it just a little longer.*
>
> *No one wants to let go of this moment but the first to break from it is DOROTHY.*

DOROTHY:       If only it had been that simple. Because wouldn't we love to tell you that we changed the world, right then and there.

POPPY:         In the movies, that's how it would go. We women would stand up to the company and the mucky-mucks would buckle at the knees – and we'd win the strike. Just like that!

KAY:           Then we'd all live happily ever after. No more injuries or illness. No money troubles. Not a care in the world.

CÉCILE:        Forever and ever, amen.

DOROTHY:       But, of course, that's not what happened.

KAY:           No. What happened after the march, for the longest time, was, well…

DOROTHY:       Nothing.

POPPY:         Company didn't budge.

KAY:    Nope. They just ignored us. Our men stayed stranded out on that picket line all through that long, bitter winter.

POPPY:    With all of us stranded there right along with 'em.

DOROTHY:    There we were, day after day, night after night, bringing coffee and whatever food we could scrounge.

CÉCILE:    But after a while that wasn't much.

*A thermos or two may be up-ended, not a drop left.*

KAY:    It got to where we had nothing left.

POPPY:    Nothing left to lose, you mean.

DOROTHY:    Oh, that's what we thought. But, as we learned, there's always, always more to lose.

*There is a sudden deep and prolonged shaking of the ground beneath their feet as we hear a long, roaring rumble. It's another rock burst – the worst one yet.*

*The women are thrown back into where they were at the time of this rock burst, in late February, 1942. Each woman braces herself and tries to hold on.*

Oh no. Oh no, oh no, oh no.

KAY:    Oh my Lord.

CÉCILE:    *Mon Seigneur.*

*POPPY totters over and falls right to the ground. A moment or two…and then the siren sounds. The women all leave at a run…except POPPY, who can't get up. She's turtled.*

POPPY:    Son of a bitch!

## Scene 13: ROCK BURST

> *The women run to the mine-head, arriving as the siren ends.*

KAY:              That's the worst one I've ever felt.

CÉCILE:           *Moi aussi.*

DOROTHY:          The house shook and shook. Felt like it would never stop.

> *POPPY waddles in last, as quickly as she's able.*

CÉCILE:           Poppy! *Fais attention.*

POPPY:            *(Catching her breath.)* Woo! Could you believe that? Felt like I was in a dollhouse someone had picked up and rattled all around. I got knocked right down – could barely get up again.

CÉCILE:           Ah, Poppy. *Viens ici.*

POPPY:            I'm fine, I promise. What are they saying so far?

KAY:              Nothing.

POPPY:            Gee, why am I not surprised?

DOROTHY:          I wonder how many men could be trapped this time. Was there a full shift on?

KAY:              No idea. And this time they're really not telling us: a bunch of strikers' wives.

POPPY:            Then where are all the scabs' wives?

CÉCILE:           Probably don't have any. Alphonse says they're barely out of diapers, those boys. Too young to go to war. Only working here to send money to their families, *hein?*

DOROTHY:    Will they have their own rescue team? The strikebreakers?

KAY:    Not a chance. They don't have the experience.

DOROTHY:    My God.

POPPY:    *(Pointing.)* Hey, those are some of our men over there – strikers – but they're letting them into the mine. Did we just win the strike somehow?

CÉCILE:    Ah *non*, Poppy. That's our mine rescue team going in.

POPPY:    What?

CÉCILE:    Our men aren't going to stand by when there are people trapped down there, no way. Somebody's got to get them out. Alphonse ran over there first thing.

KAY:    So did Bob. I bet every man on the picket line did the same – see, over there, Poppy? Isn't that your Dan over there? And there's Jim, right up there too. All of them, ready to do whatever's needed.

    *POPPY is visibly moved.*

CÉCILE:    Did you ever feel prouder to be a miner's wife?

    *A beat.*

POPPY:    With our men stepping up like that, surely they'll be earning some goodwill from the company. Do you think this could change the vote today?

CÉCILE:    I don't think so. It's over. That's the word all down the line.

| | |
|---|---|
| KAY: | The vote's just a formality now. |
| DOROTHY: | What vote? |
| KAY: | Oh, Dorothy. Jim didn't tell you. |
| DOROTHY: | Tell me what? |
| KAY: | The men are voting today. To give up the strike. |
| DOROTHY: | What? No. |
| KAY: | There's nothing else we can do. |
| DOROTHY: | No, we haven't come this far to…just to… |
| KAY: | It's been months. Long cold months. People have debts piling up. |
| CÉCILE: | People are starving. |
| DOROTHY: | All the more reason to bite the bullet. |
| CÉCILE: | Our little ones don't know about biting bullets. They only know their tummies hurt. |
| DOROTHY: | Poppy. If you talked to the men, then they'd – Poppy? |
| POPPY: | It's over, Dorothy. It is. |
| CÉCILE: | We lost, but we'll pick ourselves up. Have faith. You plant good seeds in good faith and they'll come up in good time. |
| DOROTHY: | I can't believe it. Kay, you of all people. |
| KAY: | We have to face facts. It's not working and sticking it out longer won't make any difference. The company is slowing down operations anyway so they could wait us out now 'til we've all dropped dead. |

POPPY: It's true. Danny says we've been screwed tight in a vice ever since gold mining got declared "non-essential to the war effort." The bosses will be happy to kick back for a while, sit on their golden stockpile, count their money.

DOROTHY: Even if the company's slowing things down, we don't have to. We should be stepping it up!

KAY: What good would that do? There's still no law forcing the companies to even recognize the union, never mind listen to us, never mind agree to what we're asking for.

DOROTHY: What we're *demanding!* No, they can't treat us like this. After everything we've – No!

*DOROTHY steps away from the others, then charges to the mine-head.*

*As she goes, KAY, CÉCILE, and POPPY turn to speak to the audience in the present.*

KAY: Next thing we knew, Dorothy had gone to look for the mine manager.

CÉCILE: The one who wouldn't let her get a word in the other time.

POPPY: Oh, and she found him all right. Him, and all the other stiff-necked mucky-mucks standing around in their starched collars –

CÉCILE: And her words came crashing down on them like rocks.

*DOROTHY, in 1942, to the mine manager:*

DOROTHY:   You have no right! No right to treat human beings this way. No – YOU LISTEN. YOU listen to ME! You have no right to let our husbands bleed into the rock beneath your feet and treat it like so much spit in the dust. Treat all of us like that. You're making money, hand over fist. Profits you don't know what to do with. Well, don't let that fool you, not for a second. Because no matter what profits you make – no matter how much gold you drag out from under us all – we're richer than you'll ever be. Because we haven't forgotten we're all in this together. All of us on this earth. That's why our husbands are down there helping today – that's why men who haven't had a decent meal in months are scraping through sheer rock to rescue boys you don't care about any more than you care about them. Because they know who they are. We know who we are: human beings who need each other, help each other, stand up for each other. No matter what.

*A beat – then the women applaud her, as they all shift out of that moment…*

## Scene 14: THE DUST SETTLES

*…And move into the present.*

| | |
|---|---|
| KAY: | You told 'em, Dorothy. |
| POPPY: | You sure did. |
| CÉCILE: | I was so proud of you. Speaking up like that. |
| DOROTHY: | In front of the men in charge, at last. I have to say it felt pretty good. Didn't know I had it in me. |
| KAY: | You say what needs to be said, well, it changes things. |
| DOROTHY: | Oh, it changed things, all right. It made sure Jim would never get work in Kirkland Lake ever again. Who was going to hire a man with the kind of wife who'd go and tell off the mine boss? Yeah, fat lot of good it did. |
| KAY: | Oh, it did some good. |
| CÉCILE: | You said what needed to be said. |
| POPPY: | Plus, I learned something. Never knew a man's face could turn that red! |
| KAY: | The look on him! For months, I'd picture that whenever I thought I couldn't take much more. Definitely helped. *(To the audience.)* And we needed all the help we could get. |
| CÉCILE: | Losing the strike was like the biggest rock burst of all had come crashing down on us. |
| KAY: | Knocked the wind right out of us. |
| POPPY: | Took me and Danny two years just to pay off our debt at the grocery store. |

CÉCILE:          Five years for us. Penny-pinching all the while.
                 And that's with my oldest boys helping, too.

DOROTHY:         Worst of all, losing the strike blew us all apart.

KAY.             Company bosses weren't exactly in a hurry to
                 hire back the strikers so, with everyone out of
                 work, people left town.

CÉCILE:          We stayed on – my oldest were all settled here
                 by then – but there were so many who left. It
                 was a mass exodus.

DOROTHY:         We hung on for a few months, but Jim and I
                 ended up moving back to Timmins.

POPPY:           Me and Danny went to Sudbury. Nickel City.
                 Hell, half of Kirkland Lake ended up there.
                 Nickel mining was still needed for the war
                 effort so INCO seemed a good place to try.

                 *("INCO" is pronounced "INK-o.")*

KAY:             We went to Sudbury, too.

DOROTHY:         And so fast. We hardly had a chance to say
                 goodbye.

KAY:             But we did. And, lucky for us all, you made me
                 one very important promise before we left…

## Scene 15: PROMISES, PROMISES

*DOROTHY's house, just after supper.*

DOROTHY:    Kay! Come on in!

KAY:    I can't stay, Dorothy. I've just come to say goodbye.

DOROTHY:    Goodbye? But you're not leaving 'til –

KAY:    This isn't the way I wanted to do it but we have to leave for Sudbury right now so I just want to say –

DOROTHY:    You're heading for Sudbury at this hour? It'll be pitch dark soon!

KAY:    Bob wasn't even going to stop but I insisted. I had to say goodbye to at least you. I'll see Poppy in Sudbury soon enough but you'll give my love to Cécile, won't you?

DOROTHY:    Of course I will, but you can't just leave without – this is crazy. You've got to tell Bob to come in just for a –

KAY:    You take care of yourself, Dorothy. And keep in touch. Promise me that, would ya?

DOROTHY:    Two minutes, Kay! I've got a mock apple pie coming out of the oven in just two minutes. You tell Bob to come in and at least wait for that.

KAY:    Aw, you've got a heart of gold, Dorothy, but –

DOROTHY:    My baking's much improved, I promise!

KAY:    No, hon, it's not that, it's –

DOROTHY:    And I know it sounds funny but, when you bake 'em up like that, the crackers do taste just like apples. You'll see. Jim just gobbles it up.

KAY:              No, hon, it's not that. There's just no time.

                 *A car horn honks.*

DOROTHY:          What's going on? You weren't going to be going
                 'til the end of the week.

                 *The car horn honks again.*

                 Lord, you'd think the devil was on his tail.

KAY:              We think it is. *(Off Dorothy's look.)* Couple of the
                 men showed up at the house not an hour ago
                 to warn us – some company goons are looking
                 for Bob.

DOROTHY:          But we lost the strike. Why are they after him
                 now?

KAY:              Teach him a lesson, maybe. Scare off anyone
                 else who'd ever dare utter the word "union."
                 Whatever it is, it doesn't matter. We just have
                 to get the heck out of town. Dorothy, I wish you
                 all the very, very best. Always. You take care
                 of yourself. And tell Jim to lay low for a while
                 too. Things may be tough now, but we'll get
                 through this. All of us. One way or another.

DOROTHY:          Of course we will. Aw, Kay.

                 *They embrace.*

KAY:              Promise you'll stay in touch. You've got that
                 typewriter and I want you to use it to send me
                 a letter or two.

DOROTHY:          The typewriter! I was going to find a box for it
                 but there's no time for that now. You'll take it
                 as is.

KAY:              What are you –

DOROTHY:   I want you to have it. The union's washed up here, at least for now, but you and Bob have a fresh chance to get things going in Sudbury. It could do more good there.

KAY:   No, Dorothy. Not your typewriter.

*The car horn blasts again. BOB means it this time.*

DOROTHY:   Just take it. I mean it!

*DOROTHY waves KAY to the typewriter and KAY goes to pick it up – but stops, shocked at its dead weight.*

KAY:   Oh my Lord. It weighs a ton.

DOROTHY:   It's solid, that's for sure. Could Bob –

KAY:   Bob's got a bad back and that'll finish him off for sure.

DOROTHY:   I'll call Jim –

KAY:   No, Dorothy, you keep your typewriter. And keep using it. You've got a way with words – you do. Especially when you bang 'em out on that thing. So you send along whatever news you can, whenever you can, to me, to all of us. Your Mine Mill sisters. And, hey, if you pour yourself a cup of coffee when you sit down to write and I do the same when I sit down to read what you've sent, it'll be just like we're having coffee together again. I mean, it's 1942. With the postal service and modern machines – it's amazing what's possible today. So, you promise you'll use that thing and write?

DOROTHY:   I promise.

KAY:   Now, one more hug. I gotta go!

*A quick embrace, another car horn blast, and DOROTHY sniffs something in the air as KAY dashes away…*

DOROTHY: *(Sniffing.)* Funny – it's like there's literally a fire lit under you – *(A beat and then:)* My pie! My mock apple pie!

*DOROTHY dashes away too…*

*A shift to the present. POPPY and CÉCILE rejoin them.*

CÉCILE: Funny, no one makes a mock apple pie anymore. We were so short of everything back then.

KAY: And it all seemed so final, didn't it? Like I was moving away to a foreign country.

DOROTHY: You may as well have been. Back then, no one called long distance and the drive to Sudbury's a good four or five hours.

POPPY: Me and Danny did it a hell of a lot quicker than that! I thought the wheels were going to burn right off the car the day we left.

CÉCILE: Ah, Poppy. Even now, you give my heart a shock.

POPPY: You think that's shocking? Should have seen me about a year later when I was a wartime "Rosie" working in the INCO smelter! *(Flexing her arm "Rosie the Riveter" style.)* Danny never got on there, on account of him being crippled up so, when things got desperate, I taught the fella how to change a diaper and *I* went out to work!

CÉCILE: Ah, Poppy. Good for you.

POPPY: Yeah! And I signed up union members every shift I worked too.

DOROTHY: Still, it's true. It was all so different then. When people moved away, they were gone. Sometimes, you never saw them again.

*(To POPPY and CÉCILE.)* Well, like you two. I don't think you ever...

CÉCILE: No, after you left, Poppy. I never saw you again.

POPPY: Things got so busy. But we wrote – at least that first while.

CÉCILE: You wrote. I tried. But my English...it's harder to write things down than say them.

POPPY: Didn't matter. I could feel you cheering me on.

CÉCILE: At least our goodbye was not so rushed as theirs...

*A shift back to 1942, the day POPPY and CÉCILE said their goodbyes...*

*POPPY lifts a tiny white gown out of tissue paper.*

POPPY: Oh, Cécile. It's gorgeous. Just gorgeous. That handiwork – how did you...

CÉCILE: I've had lots of practice, *hein?* I've made a few christening gowns in my time.

POPPY: Well, it's beautiful, that's what. And I'll cherish it always. Like I cherish you. I'll miss you desperately, you know. You're like a mother to me.

*CÉCILE takes POPPY's hand.*

CÉCILE: I'm so happy to have you as another daughter. And, since now you're *ma fille,* maybe you'll let me give you some advice.

POPPY:     Shoot.

CÉCILE:    Stay strong, *ma chouette*. Promise me, okay? Don't let anyone tilt your chin downward.

POPPY:     You mean, hold my head high?

CÉCILE:    *Ça s'peut.*

POPPY:     Don't you worry about that. I promise.

CÉCILE:    It's just, sometimes, especially when you become a mother, you can find you start to become someone else. Someone you think you should be, maybe. The mother you think you should be. The wife you think you should be. And when you think like that, you never feel good enough at any of it. You only see what you're not. But, *moi, là*, one thing I know – one thing I've learned – the person you are always comes out in the end anyway, so you may as well stick with that, right from the start. *Être fidèle à toi-même.* True to yourself. True to the best of yourself. And faithful to God, of course, but also true to your heart. That's what I want for you. And what I want for my little Josephine. You young girls heading into the world now, you're something, *hein?*

POPPY:     Some of you old girls are pretty great too. (*Beat.*) That didn't come out quite right. I'm not calling you old. I didn't mean to –

CÉCILE:    Ah, Poppy. *Viens-icitte!*

           *CÉCILE envelops POPPY into a huge hug.*

           *A shift…back into the present.*

           So, our goodbye, I think it was a very *good* 'bye,' *hein?*

           *CÉCILE is pleased with her pun and may wait for a reaction. She'll get it.*

DOROTHY:     And that could have been that. Us saying goodbye, losing touch with each other,

KAY:         – losing the fight.

POPPY:       Making all this just a sad story of failure: one more loss for the little guy. Not to mention, the little gal.

CÉCILE:      *Moi, là,* sometimes I think sad stories are stories that just end too soon. Like if you told about Christ, without telling about Easter.

KAY:         *(Looking at CÉCILE.)* Unshakeable.

DOROTHY:     But the truth is, we weren't done. Not quite.

KAY:         And I did get to see you again, Dorothy, just a few weeks later when I showed back up at your door in Kirkland Lake.

DOROTHY:     In the middle of the night.

## Scene 16: DRIVEN TO IT

*A shift back into late February, 1942.*

*There is a frantic banging at the door. Dorothy answers, tying on a housecoat.*

| | |
|---|---|
| DOROTHY: | What in heaven's – Kay! What are you doing back in town? |
| KAY: | I didn't know what else to do! Things have gone to pieces in Sudbury and they're looking for Bob – I didn't know where else to go! |
| DOROTHY: | Looking for – who's looking for – ? |
| KAY: | And Bob's so sick – he can barely sit up, never mind stand. Could Jim go help him in? |
| DOROTHY: | Of course he – Jim! Jim, get up!!! Bob Carson's outside and he needs some help. Now, Kay, you get in here this minute. You're freezing. |
| KAY: | There's no heater in the car. At least not that I can figure out to turn on. |
| DOROTHY: | What? *You* drove here, all the way from Sudbury? I didn't know you could drive. |
| KAY: | Me neither. |
| DOROTHY: | What's happened, Kay? |
| KAY: | What's happened is they tried to kill him! And they nearly did kill the fellas at the office! So I don't know what we do next, where we go or what's gonna happen – |
| DOROTHY: | Kay, slow down. |

KAY:     Fellow calls this morning, says there's twelve new men who want to sign up at the union hall this afternoon. And he says "make sure Carson is there." Like it has to be Bob there to sign them all up. Like he's the only one they'll trust or something. So anyway, I tell Bob but, thing is, he's ill, very ill. Still has pneumonia from being out on the picket line. So of course I don't let him go down there. Not with a temperature of a hundred-and-four! I tell Bob the other fellas in the office are perfectly capable of signing the new men up and I can go down later if he's worried, you know, to type up the papers, make sure they're done right. They do have a typewriter in the union office – we didn't need yours – and even though I can't type like you, I've been helping out some, best I can. So, anyway, I go down there this afternoon and, and the union office is on Durham Street, just over top of Levine's Ladies Wear, so, of all things, I stop a minute to stare at all the dresses I can't afford. I mean, there I am thinking about dresses. Never dreaming what's happened upstairs. But then, on my way up, I start seeing all this broken glass all over the place, all over the stairs, and blood and.... Then when I get to the office, I see the door torn right off its hinges. And everything inside is all smashed to pieces – and there's two men on the floor. Just laying there. John Whelehan and Forest Emerson. The two fellas who were going to sign the men up instead of Bob. And there they are – all bloody and gashed and Forest's neck is all twisted back so oddly...

DOROTHY:   Dear God.

KAY:          That old typewriter they have in the office –
              why, it's even bigger and older than yours, so
              what would that weigh? And they'd brought it
              down on Forest's head. John came to then, and
              here he starts moaning – I honestly couldn't
              understand what he was saying at first. Turns
              out, he's begging me to look for the list. The list.
              Before I even call for help.

DOROTHY:      The list?

KAY:          The list of miners in Sudbury who've signed
              up for the union. He was afraid the company
              thugs got away with it and that hundreds of
              men would be fired as a result. Barely alive
              and that's what he's worried about. But we
              keep that list well hidden, thank God. They
              didn't get it. I've got it with me now. *(She hugs
              herself tight.)* I'm not naive, Dorothy. I knew the
              companies were against us, against the unions.
              I knew to worry about firings, even beatings.
              But until today, I never dreamed they'd actually
              try to kill anyone.

DOROTHY:      I thought we were done, Kay, I did. That we
              just had to get back to whatever it was we were
              doing before the strike, before the march. To
              whatever we used to think was normal life.

KAY:          I don't know what normal is anymore.

DOROTHY:      Neither do I. What I do know is, we're not done.
              Not by a long shot.

## Scene 17: BACK IN ACTION

> *DOROTHY goes to the typewriter and starts to pound the keys as if her life depended on it.*
>
> *CÉCILE and POPPY reappear and, even as DOROTHY types furiously away in 1942, they all move into the present.*

KAY: You got to work that very night. Letters of protest. Letters to the editor. The write-up for the leaflet.

DOROTHY: "Murder Will Out!" Those words just came to me.

KAY: And they were perfect – our headline!

> *DOROTHY pulls the page from the typewriter.*
>
> *(A projection of the actual "Murder Will Out!" handbill could appear here.)*

CÉCILE: Jim came running over – woke me and Alphonse to tell what happened. So I brought my special make-me-well soup over for Bob. Then, while I helped Kay nurse him back to health, you took what you typed over to the printers.

KAY: Did you ever!

DOROTHY: Well, you did say to get a lot printed up.

KAY: But ten thousand copies? I couldn't believe it when you came back with all those boxes.

POPPY: *(To audience.)* Kay brought them all back with her to Sudbury and that's where me and a bunch of ladies there – and all the union fellas – well, we handed 'em all out. All ten thousand of 'em!

> *The women might leaflet the audience with copies of the actual handbill.*

DOROTHY:     I wish I'd been there.

KAY:         You were, in spirit.

POPPY:       And wouldn't you know it? *(To audience.)* I got arrested again!

CÉCILE:      *C'est pas vrai!*

POPPY:       Yeah. But not until after I'd papered the town! Plus, this time I was even less scared than the first time. I think the Sudbury police might even have been afraid of me.

CÉCILE:      Okay, Poppy. Now you're telling stories for sure.

POPPY:       You weren't there, not in Sudbury. I really came out of my shell.

CÉCILE:      *Mon Dieu.*

POPPY:       Mind you, I had my reasons.

    *A shift to POPPY, in the Sudbury police station.*

DOROTHY as
POLICEMAN:   *(With pen poised.)* Lemme get this straight. You, little lady, expect me to believe that your full and legal name is "Luck. E. Striker"?

    *POPPY may get an odd case of the giggles.*

POPPY:       Well, Officer, maybe not, but there is one thing I do expect you to believe.

DOROTHY as
POLICEMAN:   What's that?

POPPY:       You are going to let me out of here. Right now.

DOROTHY as
POLICEMAN:   Is that a fact?

POPPY:       Yep. You are going to let me out of here and you are going to take me exactly where I want to go.

| | |
|---|---|
| DOROTHY as POLICEMAN: | Really? |
| POPPY: | Mm-hmm. |
| DOROTHY as POLICEMAN: | And why would I do that? |
| POPPY: | Well, I'm not actually one hundred percent sure but I'm pretty sure…that my water just broke. |
| DOROTHY as POLICEMAN: | Your what, your water? Your water! |
| POPPY: | Okay. Now, I'm sure. Whoa!!!!!!! WHOA – OHHHHHHH!!! SON OF A – Hey, wait a sec. I'm never saying that again! |

*Beat.*

HOT DAMN!!!

*A sharp shift back to the present.*

Yep, "son of a you-know-what" just wasn't going to cut the mustard anymore so that's when I switched to saying, "Hot Damn."

| | |
|---|---|
| CÉCILE: | You could also say, "Hot Dame." |
| POPPY: | Nothing wrong with your English. |

*POPPY removes the padding she'd used to make herself look pregnant, perhaps turning it into a baby cradled in her arms.*

Anyway, that was that! Policeman forgot all about arresting me and drove me straight to the hospital. Where little Danya was born. Danya Cecile.

*CÉCILE places her hand on her heart.*

DOROTHY:     And that's not the only thing that was born that spring. All those Sudbury ladies Kay got to hand out leaflets?

CÉCILE:      She organized them into an all-new chapter of the Mine Mill Ladies Auxiliary.

DOROTHY:     And it was something!

KAY:         Local 117. Kept me busy.

             *("117" is pronounced "one-seventeen.")*

POPPY:       Me too! I was back helping with it as soon as I was able.

DOROTHY:     You kept the Kirkland Lake branch going, Cécile.

CÉCILE:      And you kept working from Timmins after you and Jim moved back there.

POPPY:       You sure did.

KAY:         You and your typewriter. Magic! Why, I think a new auxiliary chapter must have popped up every time you pounded out a newsletter!

             *DOROTHY pounds that typewriter, the words "Dear Sisters" possibly appearing as a projection.*

DOROTHY:     *(Typing.)* "Dear Sisters." That's how I'd start each newsletter I wrote. For years.

KAY:         Decades. And I'd live for them. Couldn't wait for the post.

POPPY:       Me too.

DOROTHY:     Really?

CÉCILE:      Those newsletters of yours, they kept us on track for sure. So informative. So inspiring.

POPPY:   Filled to bursting with all the news from Mine Mill Ladies across the country.

KAY:   I'd pour myself a coffee, get reading, and I could just hear you.

CÉCILE:   It was like we were all together again.

*The women read segments of DOROTHY's newsletters, with DOROTHY speaking some of the lines as they "hear" her voice… across the miles…*

*(Some of the actual typewritten newsletters could appear as projections through this.)*

POPPY:   *(Reading.)* "Auxiliary No. 131, Trail BC, with its branches at Rossland and Castlegar is doing some splendid work!"

DOROTHY:   "I enclose a sample of the leaflets these gals have been putting out recently."

POPPY:   *(Examining the leaflet.)* Way to go, girls. Nothing like leafletting!

CÉCILE:   *(Reading.)* "Marmora Auxiliary 213 could use help supplying a needy family with groceries."

DOROTHY:   "The head of the family is dying of cancer and there are nine children to support."

CÉCILE:   *(Crosses herself.)* Mon Dieu. Think of those children. We'll send help to them too.

KAY:   *(Reading.)* "We have a brand new Auxiliary at Beaverdell, BC. Word has it, they are doing a wonderful job of feeding the strikers which is starting them right off in the best Mine-Mill manner."

DOROTHY:   "The secretary there is Mrs. Gladys L. Crump. How about sending a letter of welcome to this new group?"

KAY:        *(To DOROTHY.)* I did. I bet we all did.

            *The women nod.*

POPPY:      I wrote them a bang-up letter about never losing hope! No matter what!

KAY:        *(Reading.)* "Speaking of good work – the prize has to go to Sudbury Auxiliary No. 117."

DOROTHY:    "Recently they contributed: one hundred dollars for three major strikes; twenty-five dollars to an elderly couple in trouble; fifty dollars to a sister with three small children whose husband was killed at work; and another hundred to strikers down in the states – a Christmas gift."

            *A shift back into the present.*

            All of that, out of your Sudbury local, Kay! What you did there was truly amazing.

KAY:        Well, we had a lot of women helping there.

DOROTHY:    I'll say. That Sudbury local of yours became the biggest in Canada.

POPPY:      And here they thought they'd crushed us. Ha!

KAY:        That's what happens when you get driven down deep enough. You hit gold.

CÉCILE:     We showed our true mettle. I'm using the right word?

DOROTHY:    More than the right word.

POPPY:      Once we were rolling, there was no stopping us. Any of us. We women were on the move.

KAY:        With your newsletters spreading the word, soon women just like us were setting up Mine Mill Ladies Auxiliaries absolutely everywhere.

## Scene 18: A NEW MARCH

*The women form a march formation.*

DOROTHY: From Kirkland Lake to Uranium City,

KAY: From Flin Flon to Yellowknife,

CÉCILE: And over the Rockies, right through British Columbia,

POPPY: Kimberley, Copper Mountain, all the way to Britannia Beach.

KAY: In a few short years, we had Auxiliary chapters right across Canada –

DOROTHY: Just like our sister auxiliaries had spread right across the United States.

POPPY: From Arizona to Idaho,

CÉCILE: Montana to Missouri,

KAY: And from Carlsbad, New Mexico, to Colorado, to Connecticut.

POPPY: Each of them powered by people like us.

KAY: With more joining all the time.

POPPY: We just kept dragging 'em in. Never met a crowd we didn't try to get onside.

DOROTHY: It was like our march all over again, only this time, a march through the years and right across the continent.

CÉCILE: One woman stepped up to do what she could for as long as she could. Then the next. Then the next. It was like that.

*Through the following, DOROTHY may leave the march to type up a giant list of the activities and accomplishments they name.*

*(At the same time, archival photos of their work and the many activities they name might appear projected on the sheets hanging on the clotheslines, or onto a giant stream of paper that could scroll from DOROTHY's typewriter – perhaps created from one of the sheets.)*

KAY:            We Mine Mill ladies knew how to get things done.

POPPY:          And I'll tell you one thing: we did a hell of a lot more than bake sales!

DOROTHY:        But we did those too.

CÉCILE:         Everything from sewing bees, raffles, and teas,

KAY:            To bowling nights and bazaars,

POPPY:          Even stage plays – some of us had quite a flair for the dramatic.

DOROTHY:        All to raise money – for strike relief, for injured workers, the elderly.

CÉCILE:         We sent help to people in need as far away as New Mexico.

KAY:            We gave to charities and helped build hospital wings.

DOROTHY:        We fundraised for cancer treatments,

POPPY:          Ran camps for kids,

CÉCILE:         Dance classes for children, classes for adults too,

DOROTHY:        On everything from the need to pasteurize milk, to the responsibility of jury duty.

KAY:        Education being key to a vibrant democracy.

DOROTHY:    We campaigned for women's rights,

POPPY:      And against racism.

KAY:        We lobbied hard for national health care.

POPPY:      And we got it! Good old Tommy Douglas from Saskatchewan led the charge on that one!

CÉCILE:     But how far would he have got if it hadn't been for all the women who got behind it – women who said the time had come.

DOROTHY:    Maybe best of all, we changed labour law right across the country.

*The typewriter bell rings.*

POPPY:      We did!

KAY:        We finally got the law we'd been fighting for. A law they'd had down in the States since 1935 but that we'd never had.

DOROTHY:    A law that forced companies to recognize unions. On the books in every province by 1948.

POPPY:      So they could never just ignore us, ever again.

CÉCILE:     What we went through, at Kirkland Lake – the whole country could see it was wrong. So, those seeds of justice we planted, they grew after all, *hein?*

DOROTHY:    Right into the laws and rights we have today.

KAY:        The right for workers to know what's safe and what isn't – and to make their own decisions about it.

POPPY:      The right to refuse work that's not safe.

*Looking at the list streaming out before them.*

DOROTHY:   Not bad for a bunch of miners' wives.

CÉCILE:   "By their fruits, you will know them." *(Beat.)* Did you really keep a nice long list like this, Dorothy? Of our accomplishments. So the people today, they would know about us?

DOROTHY:   Well, not exactly. But there was a list, all right, and we were all on it.

CÉCILE:   What do you mean?

## Scene 19: THE LIST

DOROTHY:   I mean, the RCMP kept that list for us. Turns out we Mine Mill Ladies were all under surveillance.

CÉCILE:   What?

POPPY:   I knew it!

DOROTHY:   All those newsletters I banged out on the typewriter? Why, the Mounties scrutinized every single one of them for signs of subversion. They watched us for close to thirty years.

KAY:   I bet our sisters in the States were under watch too.

DOROTHY:   Police kept files on us, records of everything we did – even sent spies to our meetings.

CÉCILE:   Why would the government worry about us?

KAY:   Because we were the red menace. The communist threat, incarnate!

POPPY:   *(Gesturing to CÉCILE.)* Why, if that's not the face of revolution, I don't know what is.

CÉCILE:     *Ouf!* I'm no communist.

DOROTHY:     Well, I may have gone to a few meetings.

                    *CÉCILE crosses herself.*

KAY:     Dorothy the radical! Who'd have believed it?

POPPY:     Hell, if your heart's in the right place, who cares if you're Tory blue or red as a Russian tulip on May Day? What were they so afraid of?

CÉCILE:     World takeover by bake sale?

DOROTHY:     Revolution by red velvet cake?

KAY:     Or is there just something plain scary about hard-working women who know how to get things done?

POPPY:     Touché!

CÉCILE:     All things work together for good, though, *hein?* If they hadn't kept watch on us, kept those records for reporters and scholars to find, our story might never have been told.

DOROTHY:     And we wouldn't be here now to show you who we were –

KAY:     Who we really were.

## Scene 20: EXTRAORDINARY WOMEN

DOROTHY:     Women who could stand up to the men in charge.

KAY:     *(Looking at DOROTHY.)* Women who could be the ones in charge.

CÉCILE:     Strong women. Proud women.

POPPY:      Women on the move,

DOROTHY:    On the march.

KAY:        Women who made a difference.

CÉCILE:     Women who worked together to change the world.

POPPY:      And did.

DOROTHY:    Ordinary women,

KAY:        Who weren't so ordinary, after all.

CÉCILE:     Ordinary people working together are never so ordinary, *hein?*

POPPY:      Extraordinary women.

KAY:        Is there any other kind?

DOROTHY:    So, that's who we turned out to be:

KAY:        The kind of people who can change things.

POPPY:      Like you. Every one of you.

            *The women might produce votive candles and extend them toward the audience.*

DOROTHY:    The world could still be so much safer.

CÉCILE:     And kinder.

POPPY:      It could still stand a lot more laughter.

KAY:        And a lot less fear.

DOROTHY:    It could still use you –

KAY:        Your minds,

POPPY:      Your hands,

CÉCILE:     Your hearts.

DOROTHY:        Your glowing hearts.

> *The lights dim, except for the flames that keep burning. The torch has been passed.*

*THE END.*

WITH GLOWING HEARTS
*How Ordinary Women Worked Together*
*to Change the World (And Did)*


Supplemental Material
Compiled by the Author

# Timeline of Selected Historical Events

*(Including events in the lives of some of the real-life women who inspired characters in the play)*

**1905**
Kathleen May "Kay" Carlin (née Flowers) is born in Peterborough, Ontario. (Inspiration for fictional character Kay Carson.)

**1910**
**(Oct. 27)**
Dorothy McDonald (née Bauer), long-time Mine Mill Ladies Auxiliaries coordinator, is born in Waterloo, Ontario. (Inspiration for fictional character Dorothy MacFarlane.)

**1911**
Gold is discovered in Kirkland Lake area.

**1914–1918**
World War I.

**1916**
The Western Federation of Miners becomes the International Union of Mine, Mill and Smelter Workers (IUMMSW) – a.k.a. "Mine Mill."

**1918**
**(May 24)**
Most Canadian women become eligible to vote in federal elections – except for those excluded on racial grounds. Restrictions barring Asian Canadians from voting are lifted by 1948 but First Nations women do not obtain the vote until 1960.

**1918**
**(May 22)**
Patricia "Pearl" Chytuk (née Jurczyscyn) is born in Regina, Saskatchewan. (Inspiration for fictional character Poppy Chytuk).

| | |
|---|---|
| **1928**<br>(Feb. 10) | Hollinger Mine Disaster, Timmins, Ontario. 39 killed. Leads to creation of Ontario's mine rescue program. |
| **1929** | Canadian women are recognized as persons under the law (The Persons Act). |
| **1929** | Kay (née Flowers) and Robert "Bob" Carlin marry and move to Kirkland Lake; Bob gets a job at the Teck-Hughes mine as a hoistman. |
| **1930s** | Population of Kirkland Lake grows to approximately 25,000 during the Depression as desperate people come to look for work. |
| **1930s** | In the U.S., Mine Mill Ladies Auxiliaries become intensely active in the 1930s, about a decade before Canadian auxiliaries. A Mine Mill slogan was, "A union without women is only half organized." |
| **1930**<br>(Aug. 2) | Renowned Canadian conductor and pianist Mario Bernardi is born in Kirkland Lake to parents Leone, who worked in the mines, and Rina. |
| **1931** | Estevan Coal Miners' Strike, Saskatchewan. Three killed, several injured when RCMP open fire on Sept. 29 ("Black Tuesday"). |
| **1932**<br>(June 15) | Dorothy (née Bauer) marries Jim McDonald in Kirkland Lake. |
| **1935** | Wagner Act (U.S. National Labor Relations Act) establishes union recognition in the United States. |
| **1937** | Dr. Norman Bethune visits Kirkland Lake on a fundraising drive for medical assistance for the Spanish Civil War; he stays on to help the union prepare a report on silicosis – not yet considered an industrial disease. |

| | |
|---|---|
| **1939**<br>(Sept. 1) | World War II begins. Gold mining is important to help Canada meet wartime expenditures. Canada pledges not to conscript soldiers for overseas service, although this changes by 1944. |
| **Late 1930s–1940s** | RCMP begins to keep surveillance reports on union activists for signs of communist sympathies. This includes surveillance of Dorothy McDonald and other Mine Mill Ladies Auxiliary members. |
| **1940** | In 1940, Quebec becomes the last province to allow women to vote – except those still excluded on racial grounds; in 1951, the Northwest Territories becomes the last territory to do so. |
| **1940**<br>(July 13) | Patricia "Pearl" (née Jurczyscyn) marries Dmytro "Danny" Chytuk in Wakaw, Saskatchewan. A year later, they move to Sudbury. (Unlike fictional "Poppy" Chytuk, who moves to Kirkland Lake.) |
| **1941**<br>(July) | First compulsory national unemployment system in Canada comes into operation. |
| **1941**<br>(Nov. 6) | Local newspaper reports the profits earned in 1940 by five Kirkland Lake gold mines is $13,855,000, after taxes. Miners' wages are $5.20/day. |
| **1941**<br>(July 18) | Kirkland Lake Mine Mill Union Local 240 wins unanimous approval from a government conciliation board recommending mine owners recognize and bargain with the union – but mine owners still refuse to meet with the union. |
| **1941**<br>(Nov. 18) | Kirkland Lake strike begins. Provincial police ("Hepburn's Hussars") are called in for the duration of the strike. |

| | |
|---|---|
| **1941**<br>(Nov. 26) | Possible date of Kirkland Lake women's march, organized in response to the police marches. (On Nov. 27, the local paper, *Northern Citizen*, reports a "parade" of 2,500 people the day before, comprised of "not only the striking miners but wives and children of the workmen as well.") |
| **1941** | Gold production in Canada reaches an all-time high of 166 tonnes – in subsequent years this drops sharply as wartime priorities and government policies change. |
| **1941**<br>(Dec. 7) | Bombing of Pearl Harbour. The U.S. enters the war and soon declares gold mining non-essential to the war effort, closing gold mines across the U.S. |
| **1941**<br>**(or early 1942)** | An unsigned union card is found underground at Lakeshore mine and workers are fired as a result; reported number of those fired ranges from several to more than one hundred. |
| **1941**<br>**(or early 1942)** | A rock burst at Kirkland Lake's Lakeshore mine traps replacement ("scab") workers. Mine rescue squad members (all on strike) rush to rescue the trapped men. |
| **1941** | A total of 64 men are killed in Ontario mines. Between 1917 and 1941, Ontario averaged 42 mining deaths per year. |
| **1942**<br>(Feb. 11) | Kirkland Lake strike ends; an estimated 80% of strikers are not hired back. This strike is just one of more than 1,100 work stoppages involving some 425,000 strikers between 1941 and 1943 in Canada. |
| **1942**<br>(Feb. 24) | Attack at Sudbury Mine Mill union office. Union organizers John Whelehan and Forest Emerson are badly beaten. No charges are laid. (See photo of "Murder Will Out!" leaflet.) |

| | |
|---|---|
| **1943–1980** | Mines use the inhalation of aluminum powder ("McIntyre Powder") as a measure against silicosis. Long-term health effects of this practice are now being investigated. (See mcintyrepowderproject.com) |
| **1943** | Population of Kirkland Lake is down to 15,888 after people leave town following the strike to seek work elsewhere (such as Sudbury) and to enlist. |
| **1943–1948** | Kay Carlin's husband, Robert "Bob" Carlin, serves two terms as a CCF (forerunner of the NDP) Member of Provincial Parliament for Sudbury. |
| **1944** | Sudbury Mine Mill Ladies Auxiliary Local #117 is officially chartered, although they were active well before that. |
| **1944** (March 24) | Escape by tunnel of 76 men from German P.O.W. camp Stalag Luft III; principal tunneller is former Kirkland Lake miner Wally Floody. (73 escapees are later caught, 50 are executed.) |
| **1944** | Royal Canadian Navy frigate HMCS Kirkland Lake is named after the town of Kirkland Lake in honour of the town's contributions to the war effort. |
| **1944** | Union recognition is achieved in Canada under temporary wartime Order-in-Council P.C. 1003. The Kirkland Lake strike is seen as pivotal in this. After the war, provincial legislation recognizing unions is enacted across the country by 1948. |
| **1945** | World War II ends. |

| | |
|---|---|
| **1946** | Seventeen Mine Mill Ladies Auxiliary locals are now active in Canada; this number continues to grow in the 1950s just as auxiliaries are closing south of the border. (By 1953, only eight Mine Mill auxiliaries are active in the U.S.) |
| **1947** | The Taft-Hartley Act is passed in the U.S., weakening the Wagner Act of 1935. It restricts unions' powers and also requires a guarantee that union leaders are not members of the Communist Party. |
| **1949** | Total union membership in Canada surpasses one million. |
| **1949** | Canadian Congress of Labour (CCL) expels the Mine Mill union, viewed as being swelled with communists activists, as Cold War, anti-communist climate sets in. |
| **1949** | Dorothy McDonald, national coordinator of Canada's Mine Mill Ladies Auxiliaries, is arrested and detained by U.S. police when she tries to attend a union meeting in Chicago. |
| **Mid-1950s** | With 300–400 members, the Sudbury Ladies Auxiliary local becomes the largest in Canada. (During its heyday in the 1950s, the main Mine Mill union was 100,000 strong in Canada, with 23,000 members in the Sudbury local alone.) |
| **1955** | 7th Annual Convention of Mine Mill Ladies Auxiliaries in Rossland, BC. (Dorothy McDonald is present as national chair). |
| **1958** | Workers go out on 13-week strike at Sudbury's International Nickel Company (INCO) where many former Kirkland Lake miners worked. |

| | |
|---|---|
| **1963** (April) | Date of last Mine Mill Ladies Auxiliary newsletter written by Dorothy McDonald in RCMP files. |
| **1963** | Film, *The Great Escape*, is released. Former Kirkland Lake miner Wally Floody is an advisor on the film & the real-life counterpart to the film's fictional "Tunnel King" character played by Charles Bronson. |
| **1966** | Federal government passes the Medical Care Act. Within six years, Canadians in all provinces have universal health care coverage provided on the basis of need, rather than the ability to pay. |
| **1969–1979** | The RCMP files the last of its secret surveillance reports on Sudbury's Mine Mill Ladies Auxiliary local in 1969; other union surveillance continues at least until 1979. |
| **1972** | "Right to Safety in the Workplace" legislation is enacted in Saskatchewan – the first of its kind in North America – and based in part on advice from former Mine Mill leaders familiar with the Kirkland Lake story. It enshrines three basic rights: the right to know about hazards in the workplace; the right to participate in keeping the workplace safe; the right to refuse work that is unsafe. Within a decade, similar legislation is introduced in all other provinces. |
| **1981** (Oct. 27) | Dorothy McDonald dies in Kitchener, Ontario on her 71st birthday. |
| **1984** (April 28) | First annual National Day of Mourning is held in Canada to commemorate workers who die on the job or from work-related diseases. |

| | |
|---|---|
| **1987**<br>(Mar. 4) | Agnes Gauthier, a past president of the Sudbury auxiliary, dies in Sudbury. (Partial namesake of fictional character, Cécile Gauthier, who is an amalgam and inspired by more than one person.) |
| **1988**<br>(July 10) | Kathleen May ("Kay") Carlin dies at Kirkland Lake. |
| **Late 1980s, early 1990s** | Reportedly large RCMP surveillance file on Dorothy McDonald – under surveillance for most of her life for her activism – is destroyed after being deemed of insufficient historical significance. |
| **1990** | Canada's last Mine Mill Ladies Auxiliary local – Sudbury local #117 – disbands. |
| **1993**<br>(Nov. 11–16) | In a series of articles, journalist Terry Pender of the *Sudbury Star* breaks the news of long-time RCMP surveillance of union members and activities, including those of the Mine Mill Ladies Auxiliary. |
| **2010**<br>(April 26) | Patricia "Pearl" Chytuk dies in Barrie, Ontario. |
| **Present** | To date, about 1,000 workers still die on the job or from work-related diseases every year in Canada. |

Meeting of Kirkland Lake Ladies Auxiliary #77, 1941. Dorothy McDonald stands third from the left, wearing a hat.
*(Archives of Ontario, Mike Solski fonds, F 1280-10-30, B115586, #2)*

Dorothy McDonald, circa 1940s, who devoted herself to the Mine Mill Ladies Auxiliary for two decades and was national coordinator for many years. She is the inspiration for fictional character Dorothy MacFarlane.
*(Archives of Ontario, Mike Solski fonds, F 1280-10-1-31, B115586, #77)*

Dorothy McDonald with Kirkland Lake Union Local 240 President William Simpson, shortly after the strike was called off in 1942.
*(Laurentian University Archives. P035 Nelson Thibault fonds. Series: Mine Mill Union Photographs)*

Ladies Auxiliary (L.A.) reps of northeastern Ontario meet in Sudbury, early 1940s. Dorothy McDonald is 4th from the left; Kay Carlin is at the centre of the table. Kay Carlin, the first L.A. organizer in Canada, is the inspiration for fictional character Kay Carson.
*(Archives of Ontario, Mike Solski fonds, F 1280-10-1-30, Box B115586, #1)*

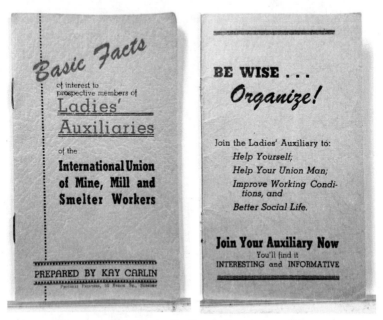

Ladies Auxiliary pamphlet prepared by Kay Carlin – cover and first page.
*(Archives of Ontario, Mike Solski fonds, F 1280-18, File 3, Box B253516)*

Kirkland Lake Strike, 1941– picket line duty. Strikers used the tents as shelter before police tore them down and banned mass picketing.
(*Archives of Ontario, Mike Solski fonds, B115588, 1.32*)

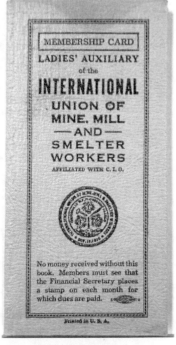

Miners 3000–4000 feet underground at Lakeshore mine, Kirkland Lake, circa 1940. Photographs were not allowed but this shot was captured by miner Gordon Henderson.
(*Museum of Northern History, Kirkland Lake, #2007.3.15*)

Mine Mill Ladies Auxiliary membership card.
(*Archives of Ontario, Mike Solski fonds, F 1280-18, File 4, Box B253516*)

Ladies Auxiliary members gathering donations with Agnes Gauthier on right. A past president of Sudbury L.A. #117, Agnes Gauthier is the partial namesake of fictional character Cécile Gauthier. (Photo undated)
*(Archives of Ontario, Mike Solski fonds, F 1280-10-1-30, B115586, #9)*

Sudbury Mine Mill Ladies Auxiliary gathering Easter parcels, 1957. Standing at centre is longtime union activist Pearl Chytuk, the inspiration for fictional character "Poppy" Chytuk.
*(Archives of Ontario, Mike Solski fonds, F 1280-10-1-30, B115586, #37)*

Ontario Provincial Police "Hepburn's Hussars" stand at attention, ready to march.
*(Archives of Ontario, Mike Solski fonds, F 1280-10-1-12, B115584, Sheet 3.5)*

Ontario Provincial Police "Hepburn's Hussars" on the march during the strike.
*(Archives of Ontario, Mike Solski fonds, F 1280-10-1-12, B115584, Sheet 3.5)*

Kirkland Lake women gather for a march of their own, 1941.
*(Archives of Ontario, Mike Solski fonds, F 1280-10-1-40, Box B115588, #1.25)*

Kirkland Lake women march through town, 1941.
*(Archives of Ontario, Mike Solski fonds, F 1280-10-1-40, B115588, #1.27)*

The women just keep coming.
*(Archives of Ontario, Mike Solski fonds, F 1280-10-1-40, B115588, #1.28)*

The women continue on, down Government Road.
*(City of Greater Sudbury Heritage Images, Solski Collection, ID# MK2344)*

The women of Kirkland Lake, leading the way.
*(Archives of Ontario, Mike Solski fonds, F 1280-10-1-40, B115588, #1.30)*

With a crowd of striking miners, following in their footsteps.
*(Archives of Ontario, Mike Solski fonds, F 1280-10-1-40, B115588, #1.23)*

Kirkland Lake strikers, 1941.
*(Archives of Ontario, Mike Solski fonds, F 1280-10-1-12, B115584, #3.4)*

Members of the Sudbury Ladies Auxiliary helping in kitchen; on the right is Pearl
Chytuk. In the 1950s, Sudbury #117 became the largest L.A. local in Canada.
*(UBC Special Collections, International Union of Mine, Mill and Smelter Workers
[Canada] fonds, Box 3, File BC1449-117y)*

Ladies Auxiliary delegates at the 8th Canadian Convention of the Mine Mill union, Sudbury, Feb. 27, 1956. Dorothy McDonald, longtime national coordinator of Mine Mill Ladies Auxiliaries, is seated, second from the right
*(Reprinted from* Mine Mill *by Mike Solski and John Smaller. Used with permission.)*

Dorothy McDonald, still going strong as a union activist in the 1960s.
*(Archives of Ontario, Mike Solski fonds, F 1280-10-1-31, Box B115586, #78)*

Kay's husband Bob Carlin was elected as Sudbury's C.C.F. Member of Provincial Parliament in 1943. Here, Kay and Bob Carlin (on right) meet in Sudbury with (on left) Victor Whelan (President, C.C.F. Sudbury) and Claire Gillis (C.C.F. M.P. for Cape Breton), May 1943.
*(Archives of Ontario, Mike Solski fonds, F 1280-10-1-1, Container B115581, #1.24)*

Ladies Auxiliary locals opened across the country. Here Ladies Auxiliary
members in Trail, BC demonstrate in support of the Mine Mill union,
May 12, 1952.
*(Laurentian University Archives. P035 Nelson Thibault fonds.*
*Series: Mine Mill Union Photographs)*

Mine Mill Ladies Auxiliaries worked to support many causes and charities.
Pictured here is the Mobile Unit of the Canadian Arthritis and Rheumatism
Society, sponsored by Mine Mill Local 598, Sudbury, 1953.
*(Archives of Ontario, Mike Solski fonds, F 1280-10-1-40, B115588, #1.13)*

Mine Mill Ladies Auxiliary "Program for the Coming Year" (undated).
Listed priorities are: 1) Support of parent organization; 2) Price control,
3) Political action and legislation (PAC Leg's); 4) Organization; 5 (missing);
6) Child care; 7) Teen age problems, 8) Community work; 9) Health;
10) Housing; 11) Racial problems; 12) World peace.
*(Archives of Ontario, Mike Solski fonds, F 1280-18, File 5, Box B253516)*

**PROGRAM OF MINE- MILL AUXILIARIES**

1: Support of our parent organiation both morally and financially.

2: Price control and consumer problems.

3: Political action and legislation.

4: Organiation.

5: Child care.

6: Education.

7: Teenage problems and nurseries.

8: Community work.

9: Health.

10. Housing

11. Racial problems.

12. Active work for world peace.

Mine Mill Ladies Auxiliary program of work as it later appears in a newsletter
from late 1951 or early 1952. The missing item in the previous handwritten list
appears here as "Education."
*(UBC Special Collections, International Union of Mine, Mill and Smelter Workers*
*[Canada] fonds, Box 94, File 15, Newsletter No. 120)*

# MURDER WILL OUT!

To all citizens and workers of Sudbury we present the true facts concerning the murderous, storm-trooper raid on the Durham Street office which took place Tuesday, February 24th. Behind it was the fascist hand of INCO - - - as we all have suspected. Where did we get the truth? From two of the degenerates who sold out all principle, all honor, all Canadianism, to INCO, and stooped beneath the level of Huns - - - from two of the "loyal workers" who took part in the attempted massacre of two union organizers.

The affair was engineered by Harry Smith, Superintendent of the Frood Mine - - - establishing the whole thing as a viscious INCO plot. Here are seven of the Frood scum who made the raid. There were twelve altogether - - - against two peaceful men in a quiet office. Two of these seven have talked.

**GORCE, Louis**     **STILLMAC, Stinky**
**FORAN, Jack**     **O'MALLEY, George**
**McKAY, Neil**     **LINDSEY, Tom**
**JOHNSTON, Jack**

Fuehrer Harry Smith told the above - - - and, note the stope bosses - - - to "go the limit" in wrecking the office and everything in it. He told them to "do a good job on the organizers". He told them "not to worry about broken bones or smashed teeth or anything like hospital bills". He told them they wouldn't get caught "because the police would be someplace else at the time". He told them "not to worry about getting back on the job - - - your pay will continue". This is the violence that INCO and their blowzy prostitute "Sudbury Star" blame on the union.

And, as a Sudbury policeman - - - a "guardian of law and order" - - - later remarked, "they sure did a GOOD job". Well, Hitler would call it good - - - it's what he ordered. Whelehan - - - a citizen of Sudbury for over fifteen years - - - was beaten unmercifully with fists and furniture. Emerson - - - an American citizen of Canadian parentage - - - had his head laid open with a cudgel and was beaten with anything they could pick up. Both got the boots when they were half unconcious and bleeding profusely on the floor. Either could have been killed.

The unspeakable "Sudbury Star" has been editorially demanding why the men don't go into court and prove it. The answer is that the men who did this dirty work between 5:15 and 5:30 p.m. were punched in at the mine for the four o'clock shift. INCO had nice alibis all prepared.

**This may be what INCO wants - - - it may be what the Star wants - - - but it is not what we want, and not what Sudbury wants. We are not going to stand for this kind of a deal. We are fighting for democracy abroad. We do not propose to accept fascism here in Canada and the above is plain Hitler fascism, and nothing else.**

We want better wages, hours and working conditions. We want security and seniority recognition on the job. We want a lot of things so far denied to us by INCO - - - and, ABOVE ALL, we want decency and democracy in Canada. Neither INCO nor anybody else can prevent us from being true Canadians - - - and fighting for what we know is right.

# THIS BETTER NOT HAPPEN AGAIN

## Rank and File Sudbury Miners and Smeltermen

"Murder Will Out!" leaflet written in Kirkland Lake following the attack on the Sudbury union office on February 24, 1942; 10,000 copies were made and handed out in Sudbury.
*(Reprinted from* Mine Mill *by Mike Solski and John Smaller. Used with permission.)*

## *You can work for a better future for your family!*

### Through the MM Ladies' Auxiliary ...

Members are the wives, mothers, sisters and daughters of Mine Mill members throughout Canada. The Auxiliary helps the Union carry out its program—for lower prices, health and welfare plans, wage increases, against unemployment, for increased educational facilities for children, slum clearance, adequate housing, against discrimination of all kinds and for peace and security.

### We know you're busy, but ...

If Mine Mill has no Ladies' Auxiliary in your area, how about helping to get one started? You will find that your activity counts as much as your husband's, father's, son's, or brother's in making the Union stronger. A stronger Union means a better life for Mine Mill members and their families. A stronger Union, a stronger Auxiliary means that folks like us will have stronger defense against the power of the huge corporations. Without the Union, the companies have things their own way ALL of the time. And the employees and their families find the going tougher and tougher.

### You can help your men ...

By working with other women in your community to explain why the Union is so important to working people. You can help plan recreational and social activities for the local union. You can help the local union in its legislative campaigns. You can help it establish better relations with the rest of the community. You can carry the UNION MESSAGE to other workers' groups, to church organizations and civic bodies.

### You can help your kids ...

By joining with other union women and men to obtain better school facilities, free hot lunch programs for school children, better recreational facilities for boys and girls in your community. You can help combat juvenile delinquency by substituting wholesome activities for the corner gang.

### You can help yourself ...

By learning the fundamentals of trade unionism and getting better understanding of the program and objectives of Mine Mill. You can learn, as trade unionists have had to learn, that a better life for you depends upon COLLECTIVE ACTION. Whether you want a home to call your own, healthier and happier kids, or fewer financial worries, the Ladies' Auxiliary is the place for you.

HERE ARE WORTHWHILE OBJECTIVES FROM MINE MILL CONSTITUTION

Mine Mill Ladies Auxiliary promotional card (Side 1).
(*Archives of Ontario, Mike Solski fonds, F-1280-15, Box B253516*)

## OBJECTS
### FROM MINE MILL CONSTITUTION

The objects of this organization shall be to unite the various persons working under our jurisdiction into one central body, to practise those virtues that adorn society and remind man of his duty to his fellow men and

To improve general conditions by increasing wages and shortening hours of labor;

To improve working conditions by removing or preventing the dangers incident to our work;

To eliminate the dust, smoke, gases, poisonous fumes and improving ventilation and lighting systems in our working places;

To labor for the enactment of legislation that will protect the lives and limbs of the workers, and conserve their health;

To improve the social conditions of the workers and their families;

To negotiate agreements with our employers and by lawful means, establish the principles embraced in the body of this constitution;

To promote political action consistent with democratic principles.

We hold these ends may be obtained by legislation and political action, negotiation, joint agreements, or strikes, in securing better conditions, better compensation for the workers' labor, by encouraging and interesting them in the study of economic, political and industrial questions.

We extend to all workers who rightfully come under the jurisdiction of "The Union" without regard to race, religion, or political belief, color or nationality, an invitation to unite with us that these ends may be attained.

*You Too Can Help Achieve These Worthwhile Aims Through Your Ladies' Auxiliary*

Write to:

AUXILIARY COORDINATOR
INTERNATIONAL UNION OF MINE MILL
& SMELTER WORKERS (CANADA)
1219 QUEEN ST. W., TORONTO 3

OR CONTACT YOUR LOCAL UNION OFFICERS

Dear Mrs. McDonald:

Please send me additional information on the Ladies' Auxiliary.

NAME ........................................

ADDRESS ...................................

My husband is a member of Mine Mill Local No. ..............

INTERNATIONAL UNION OF MINE MILL
& SMELTER WORKERS (CANADA)

# THERE MUST BE SOMETHING
## YOU CAN DO ABOUT IT ...

**IF** HIGH PRICES have you worried and you find it impossible to make ends meet.

**IF** THE TOWN in which you live needs better improvements, better streets, parks, recreation, hospital, better municipal government.

**IF** YOU WISH to assist your husband in his fight to improve your family's standard of living.

**IF** YOU WANT to know what the UNION is trying to do ...

THEN THIS IS IMPORTANT
—IT AFFECTS YOU AND
YOUR FAMILY

Mine Mill Ladies Auxiliary promotional card (Side 2).
*(Archives of Ontario, Mike Solski fonds, F-1280-15, Box B253516)*

# For More Information

## Books

*Mine Mill: The History of the International Union of Mine Mill and Smelter Workers in Canada since 1895,* by Mike Solski & John Smaller. Ottawa: Steel Rail Publishing, 1984. ISBN 0-88791-029-7 (paper); ISBN 0-88791-031-9 (hardcover).

*Whose National Security? Canadian State Surveillance and the Creation of Enemies.* Editors: Gary Kinsman, Dieter K. Buse, & Mercedes Steedman. Toronto: Between the Lines Press, 2000. ISBN 978-1-89635-725-6 (paperback); ISBN 978-1-92666-274-9 (e-pub). Contains many interesting articles, including two with particular relevance to this story:

  – Mercedes Steedman's "The Red Petticoat Brigade, Mine Mill Women's Auxiliaries and the Threat from Within, 1940s–1970s," 55–71.

  – Julie Guard, "Women Worth Watching: Radical Housewives in Cold War Canada," 72–88.

*Hard Lessons: The Mine Mill Union in the Canadian Labour Movement.* Editors: Mercedes Steedman, Peter Suschnigg and Dieter Buse. Toronto: Dundurn Press, 1995. ISBN 978-1-55002-223-0 (paperback); ISBN 978-1-45972-598-0 (e-pub).

*Remember Kirkland Lake: The Gold Miners' Strike of 1941–42, Revised Edition* by Laurel Sefton MacDowell. Toronto: Canadian Scholars' Press, 2001. ISBN 1-551-30-159-8.

## Articles

"Textually Mediated Labour Activism: An Examination of
the Ladies Auxiliary of the Canadian Mine Mill & Smelter
Workers Union, 1940s–1960s," by Elizabeth Quinlan and
Andrea Quinlan. (2015) *Journal of International Women's Studies*
16(3): 137–157.
Available at: http://vc.bridgew.edu/jiws/vol16/iss3/10

"RCMP spied on conventions and women's auxiliaries," *Sudbury
Star*, Nov. 13, 1993, p. B4. (Part of a series of news-breaking
articles that ran Nov. 11–16, 1993 by Terry Pender.)

## Other

"The Ladies Auxiliary of the Mine Mill and Smelter Workers
Union (Canada) 1940s–1960s," presentation by Andrea Quinlan
and Elizabeth Quinlan. Available at:
https://youtu.be/whAKutkhmWI

More information and various videos of and about the play,
including *With Glowing Hearts: Academic Page to Popular Stage*,
a short feature about the making of the play, are available at:
www.jenniferwebber.com/With-Glowing-Hearts

Charlie Angus/Grievous Angels song, "Having to Say Goodbye,"
at: https://youtu.be/5rO0kdoM8OE
(Includes archival photos and film footage of Kirkland Lake)

Historical film footage of Kirkland Lake at:
https://youtu.be/6dlLlG-y06w

More archival film footage of Kirkland Lake: "Lake Shore Mine,
1937" on YouTube at:
https://www.youtube.com/watch?v=InQygl-kBtE

Mine Mill Ladies Auxiliary Newsletters, typed by Dorothy McDonald, are available at:

– UBC Special Collections, International Union of Mine, Mill and Smelter Workers (Canada) fonds.

– Library and Archives Canada, Ottawa, Public Access, RG 146, Vol. 119, File AH2001-00070. (An Access to Information Act request is no longer required to view these files because of the request in 1992 by the *Sudbury Star* which released some 9,000 pages of material from previously confidential RCMP files.)

Interviews with former Mine Mill Ladies Auxiliary members (such as Kay Carlin) and other related materials are available at: Laurentian University Archives: P211 Elizabeth Quinlan Collection; P047 Barbara Dunphy fonds; and P144 Mercedes Steedman fonds.

www.elizabethquinlan.net

www.jenniferwebber.com